Hills, Skills, and Wills

How to Improve
Your (and Others) Performance

Michael J. Ayulo

Copyright© 2013 Michael J. Ayulo

All rights reserved.

ISBN: 978-0-9899932-1-0

DEDICATION

To Tim: I miss you!

CONTENTS

Acknowledgments		9
1.	Introduction	11
2.	Performance, Expectation, and Performance Gaps	17
3.	Human Behavior and the Most Important Question	23
4.	Hills, Skills, and Wills	37
5.	True Stories	49
6.	How to Resolve the Gaps	59
7.	Process and Practice	71
8.	Conclusion and Next Steps	97
Appendix A		103
Appendix B		111

ACKNOWLEDGMENTS

I would like to express my gratitude to those who stuck with, encouraged, and helped me through the writing of this book.

Thanks to my wife, Kirsten, and our children Abby and Cooper, who supported and encouraged me through the process.

I would also like to thank Steve Pechter, Juliet Evans, Michael Sciarra, Cam Danielson, Brian Miller, and my wife Kirsten for being my sounding boards, challenging my thinking, offering their comments, and helping me in the process of editing and/or proofreading.

Thanks to Tanya Wlodarczyk for your guidance in getting this book to publication and my daughter, Abby, for her artistic contributions.

I must also thank all those whose performance behaviors I have learned from over the years, both good and bad.

Last, and as far from least as possible, I would like to thank God for keeping this project on my mind/heart for so long and for pushing me to finally do it. Use it in the lives of whoever, however, you see fit!

1. INTRODUCTION

Every day people and organizations try to improve their peformance. Businesses focus on getting their employees to do their jobs better and/or faster. They seek to improve their technologies and products, or streamline their processes and tactics. Likewise, we as individuals do the same. We try to make more money, improve our golf swing, lose a few pounds, spend more time with our children, or some other venture. Sometimes companies and organizations refer to these performance improvement actions as "strategic initiatives" while in our personal lives, we may simply refer to them as trying to "turn over a new leaf."

Unfortunately, many of these attempts to improve performance fail. Individuals and organizations spend hundreds, thousands, millions, even billions of dollars trying to change our (or others) performance from where it is, to where we want it to be, only to find that after all was said, spent, and done, there was little to no change that actually took place. Company profits continue to decline, individuals continue to gain weight, and a host of other changes that well-intentioned people seek to achieve never take place. Why do performance issues exist and why do we so often fail to resolve them? In every situation where performance is falling short or failing to change, there are three words that explain the reason. They are easy to remember and clearly point where your problem solving efforts should be focused. Would you like to know what they are?

They are; Hills, Skills, and Wills.

Every gap in performance since the beginning of time has been, or is being, caused by one or more of these three words, and the reason(s) individuals, companies, organizations, and countries frequently fail to resolve them is because we jump into implementing solutions without first knowing which of these three performance killers is the true cause of the problem.

It is heartbreaking to watch people and organizations fail in improving or changing their performance simply because they didn't understand the possible causes and then rushed into implementing half-baked solutions, but to add further insult to this injury, many of these misguided attempts to improve performance are never even evaluated to see if they actually worked. This is more often true in organizations, as personal failures are more difficult to ignore (though it is certainly possible). Having worked with organizations for over three decades now, I have witnessed an increasing number of organizational leaders discount, disguise, or simply ignore evaluation of their performance efforts. The reasons for this vary but include things like; lack of time, lack of ability, fear of losing their job, and in the worst cases, ego and the leader's complete inability to even entertain the thought that their solutions would result in anything less than success. Regardless of the reasons, Hills, Skills, and Wills are always at the root of every performance problem and every refusal to address or correct them.

The primary purpose of this book is to provide you with the knowledge and tools to identify the Hills, Skills, and Wills behind any performance gap, develop solutions that target these specific gaps, and achieve the performance improvements you desire or need. In the remainder of this introduction, you will take a short self assessment that will start you thinking about any performance gaps you may be currently experiencing, as well as help you decide, in the case that you are reading this intro at the bookstore, whether this book is worth purchasing. I will also give you a little background on myself that may answer the question… why should I listen to this guy? Before I do this, however, let me provide you with a brief overview of each chapter in the book.

In Chapter 2, we will define and discuss performance, performance improvement, and the connection between it and behavioral expectations. I will explain how performance gaps require behavioral change and provide some real-life examples that demonstrate what can happen when people do not understand the information you will be learning in this book.

In Chapter 3, you will confront and answer the first and most important question that anyone who wants to be successful in improving performance must answer. In order for you to better answer that question, we will also discuss a little bit about human behavior and how it relates to performance. Finally, I will challenge your thinking and share some more real-life examples that will solidify your answer and serve as the cornerstone for all your future performance improvement efforts, whether in the business world or in your personal life.

In Chapter 4 and 5, we will get to the root cause of all performance gaps; Hills, Skills, and Wills. I'll show how correctly identifying those gaps is the key to performance improvement, provide easily relatable business and personal examples, and share two cases that demonstrate how this plays out in real life.

In Chapter 6, we begin to shift our focus from understanding and identifying the cause of the performance gaps to developing targeted solutions. Ultimately, there is no limit to the number of solutions that could be developed but there are certain approaches that have proven to increase success when confronting Hill, Skill, or Will gaps. This chapter will discuss those approaches and prepare you for using them in the next.

In Chapter 7, we will take what we have learned about human behavior, the cause of the performance gaps, approaches to developing targeted solutions, and I will introduce and walk you through a job aid that you can use to identify the causes and develop solutions for your own performance improvement needs.

In the Conclusion, we will wrap things up and check whether I have accomplished what I pledged to do. More importantly, I will explain what you can do next. How you can join with others who are interested in conducting their own performance related experiments, sharing their results, and working together to prove, disprove, refine, and/or revise what has been learned by applying it in their worlds.

Is This The Right Book For You?

Not to be matter-of-fact but let's face it, before you invest your time or money in buying this book, you probably want an answer to one of the key questions that drives our behavior as human beings, "What is in it for me?" Let's answer this question quickly. Below is a short self assessment. Start by reading each question in the assessment and place a checkmark next to each one that applies to you personally. After you have added your checkmarks, count up the total number of checkmarks and write it down in the space provided at the bottom of the list.

If you only placed a checkmark next to one of these questions, you're still in the right place. Of course, the more checkmarks you have, the more relevant and helpful this book will be to you. My pledge and expectation is that by the end of this book, you will not only be able to look at any performance gap and quickly identify what has been keeping you from being able to change it, but you will be able to create a plan that will specifically target those causes and help you, or your organization, succeed in achieving the performance you so desire or need.

- ☐ Is there something that you would like to change about yourself?
- ☐ Is there something that you would like to change about someone else?
- ☐ Have you ever tried to change something about yourself but keep failing in your attempts?
- ☐ Would it be helpful if you could pinpoint exactly why you continue to fail in your attempts to change?
- ☐ Would being able to quickly and easily find the best way to stay on track in accomplishing your goal be useful to you?
- ☐ Would comparing, sharing, and monitoring your results and efforts with others who are also looking to make changes be helpful?

TOTAL _____

Who Am I That You Should Listen To Me?

If you are anything like me, it is important to know something about the person giving you advice. Understanding their interest in a topic, where that interest comes from, and what experience they have, helps determine just how much credibility I place on what they tell me.

My most important (and really only important) credential is that I am someone who has personally walked the talk. While I live in California, I greatly appreciate the Missouri state slogan; Missouri is the "Show Me" state. I don't think I could write or tell others to do something if I was not sure it worked and had successfully tested it in my own life. For nearly two decades now, I have practiced and succeeded in identifying, developing, and implementing performance solutions by understanding and using the information I have detailed in this book. I consider myself to be a pretty average guy, but here are a few things about me and my personal experiences and background that you may find relevant and may help build your confidence that what I am sharing warrants your continuing to read this book.

I have always been fascinated and naturally curious with the way people behave and why they do what they do. As far back as I can remember, this has resulted in my purposeful watching and talking with the people I have encountered about their behaviors, and the reasons behind them.

I was also a vocational minister for several years (and continue to do as a volunteer). As such, I have not only studied the social and psychological reasons for people's behaviors but I have examined and struggled with the spiritual/theological aspects of them. I have interacted, debated, and counseled with people from several countries, from all walks of life, and from many different faiths (or non-faiths). I have seen firsthand just how much this spiritual aspect is, to varying degrees, shared by the overwhelming majority of human beings and how it drives our behavior and performance at various times in our lives.

I, in no way, consider myself an academic but I do hold several scholarly degrees. I hold a Bachelor's degree, a Master's degree, and completed most but not all of my Doctoral dissertation. I do not mention these to toot my academic horn, but rather to explain that all of these studies have all concentrated in the fields of Education and Behavioral or Social Studies. This has helped by introducing me to various theories that I could reflect upon, observe, hold up, and test against my understanding of performance improvement and the reality of behaviors by everyday people in everyday situations and environments.

Finally, I have spent more than two decades working for, and with, organizations as a Human Capital Management expert. Now you might say, "that's an interesting title," what is a Human Capital Management expert? Well, as you might expect, companies focus the majority of their time and effort managing their "capital," the products, assets, and money that define them as a business. However, no company can survive without its "Human

Capital," the people that make the products, maintain the assets, or manage the money. Companies cannot survive without their human capital, and while some do an excellent good job at ensuring their people are valued just as highly as their finances, products, and materials, there are plenty that do not. In these companies they may say all the right things but their actions, and the results of those actions, speak otherwise.

This has been the professional space I've played in. In companies ranging from small, private Dot-Coms, to Fortune 50 companies, to companies with employees in over 60 countries worldwide, I have partnered with business leaders regarding the behavior of their employees and the enormous value or problems they can bring when appropriate attention is or is not given to them. I have analyzed and identified potential solutions, and then implemented them in ways that have succeeded beyond what was hoped for, as well as ways that, unfortunately, failed. In working with these organizations I have also gained a deep understanding and expertise in how businesses function. With this experience and expertise, I have married the two into a private practice called Cornerstone Business and Executive Coaching. Here, I now work exclusively with business owners and executives that just sometimes get stuck. They get stuck on both the tactical and human sides of their businesses. Things like lack of profitability, lack of sales growth, employee retention problems, or simply working too many hours and still not being any closer to their goals. In short, I coach them on how they can improve their personal performance and the performance of their businesses.

So there you have it. In a nutshell:

- The book is about improving performance.
- All performance gaps are caused by Hills, Skills, and Wills, and your solutions need to target the right ones.
- If you want to improve your performance, and scored at least a 1 on the self assessment, this book is for you.
- When it comes to understanding and improving performance, this is not my first time around the block.

2. PERFORMANCE, EXPECTATIONS, AND PERFORMANCE GAPS

In chapter 3 we will discuss Hills, Skills, and Wills, their importance, and how to quickly identify these performance killers. However, before we do so, we need to do two things. First, we need to define some basic terms and concepts, and then we will need to address the most important question that everyone seeking to improve performance must first answer. In this chapter we will focus on the first of these two requirements, addressing the terms and concepts. This will ensure we are speaking the same language and help you more easily understand how they all connect and work together toward improving performance. I will also provide some examples, showing how people and businesses frequently waste their energy and resources by not understanding these concepts or how to apply them appropriately.

PERFORMANCE AND PERFORMANCE EXPECTATIONS

First, we need to clearly understand what is meant by the term "Performance." Merriam-Webster's[1] dictionary defines performance as:

1. The execution of an action,
2. The fulfillment of a claim, promise, or request.

Simply put, it is what we DO. It is how we behave. It is how we act and react to the situations in our lives and environments.

---

1   Merriam-Webster. February 10, 2013. <http://www.merriam-webster.com/>

To illustrate this, look at the table below and note the actions, behaviors, and performance of the following people:

Performer	Performance
An actor in a play	Delivers their lines
A singer on stage	Sings a song
An athlete on the field	Catches the ball
A doctor in the operatng room	Removes a tumor
A high school student	Attends classes

These examples show the simplicity of this concept but they also help illustrate a second, foundational concept that we need to understand when discussing performance. *Performance is always tied to an expectation.*

When people fail to execute or fulfill actions in the way we expect them to, we label that performance as poor or unsatisfactory. Think about it. We expect actors to portray their characters in a way that makes us believe they really are that other person, and not simply "acting" as that other person. When they succeed, we say that they gave a great performance. When they don't succeed, we label them as poor actors and their performance as poor. We expect singers to sing on key. We expect doctors to remove tumors without killing the patient or causing other damage. We expect high school students (especially if they are our sons or daughters) to attend their classes. Even something as mundane as drinking a cup of coffee carries an expected performance...that:
- We will like the taste of it
- It won't be too hot or too cold
- It won't spill all over us
- It is not too expensive

The expectations associated with performance may be those that you have of yourself, they may be your expectations of someone else, or someone else's expectation of you, but every performance is tied to, and judged according to, some expectation.

Unfortunately, the expectations connected with performance can be complex. Some, like those I shared in the list, are pretty straight forward and are generally shared by all. However, performance expectations can change significantly depending on the context (people and situations). For example, let's consider a situational context. The performance expectations for a child in a kindergarten play are very different than the expectations for a teenager in a civic theater production, and those are very different than the expectations for someone in a Broadway musical. Each venue (situation) will impact the expectations of those experiencing it. Now let's consider how performance expectations may vary depending on the context of the people involved. For example, a 10-year-old may have a very different expectation for drinking a cup of coffee. He or she may expect it to taste more like a cup of hot chocolate or to be sipped through a straw. In looking at the example of a actor, not only will the age and skill level of the actor affect the expectations, but your personal expectations may be different than mine, mine may be different than someone else's, and both of ours may be different than the actor's himself/herself. These expectations can spring from one's culture, life experiences, and a host of other influences. For instance, in 2012, I was in a major U.S. city with a group of coworkers and decided to go to the city theater's opening night presentation of the musical "Wicked." I had already seen the show in Los Angeles, twice, and loved it. Others had never seen it. By the end of the show I could easily see that we all had very different expectations. One person in our group slept through most of the show. Another was frustrated because some of the climactic scenes were altered (like me, she obviously had seen the show elsewhere before). Still others came out enthusiastically praising the performance. We all saw the same performance but we all had several different expectations.

This aspect of performance expectations is actually one of the culprits behind many failed business initiatives. People assume that others' expectations are the same as theirs, and they frequently fail to take the time to make sure what they expect is the same as others. Can you imagine the end result of those situations? It's like watching a soccer game where each team has a different set of rules to play by. I see this over and over again. Ten business leaders can sit in the same room and all agree that they expect their employees to "understand the company values." The problem is, they all have different expectations of what it means to "understand." For some, it means to simply tell the employees what the values are. For others, it means to make sure they know what they are and can repeat them back to someone if asked. For still others, it means that the employees will enthusiastically embrace, live, eat, and breathe them in their daily interactions.

Whether it is "understanding" the company values or some other business expectation, I have seen good, well-intentioned people spend large sums of time and money to create solutions that will meet expectations and then, only afterwards, find out that their expectations about what "understand" means were very different.

Now some leaders have skilled Human Capital professionals that they trust and partner with to clarify and address these issues up front. Unfortunately, others do not, and I have experienced and heard far too many instances where the Human Capital professional tries to clarify expectations only to be reprimanded or criticized for wasting time in analysis, that the leaders are too busy with other matters, or that they expect you to tell them what it means to "understand _____" (which may still be different than what they expect). Performance expectations will vary depending on the context but regardless, there is always an expectation tied to performance.

PERFORMANCE GAPS

Another definition or concept that we need to be clear about is that of a performance gap. When people's actions do not match their (or someone else's) expectations, the difference between what was expected and what actually happens is referred to as a performance gap. For example, let's say you purchased a new weight loss drug that claims you will lose 50 pounds without having to change your diet. You make the purchase and faithfully follow the instructions prescribed on the bottle, but you only lose 30 pounds. In this case, the performance gap is 20 pounds because the difference between 50 pounds (what was expected) and 30 pounds (what actually happened) is 20 pounds. Likewise, let's say you manage a team of sales people. You expect each of your salespeople to close 1 million in new business each quarter, but the best sales person is only closing 500 thousand and the worst is closing 100 thousand each quarter. In this scenario, the difference (the performance gap) is 500 thousand – 900 thousand in new business sales, per salesperson, per quarter.

CHANGE IS REQUIRED

The last definition or concept to be clear about is that every solution to a performance gap requires change. Without change, performance gaps will remain and no improvements will ever be achieved. Furthermore, it is not enough to simply make a change; the changes made must be the right one(s). I have seen and heard of some phenomenal cases where people made the right changes and experienced incredible improvements as a result. Unfortunately, we have all heard or seen stories of people whose lives continue to spiral out of control (fail to improve their performance) because they refuse to see and make the right changes. This is, perhaps, even more prevalent within organizations.

As previously discussed, people can have differing expectations regarding a particular performance, and since organizations, by definition, include more than one person, seeing and making the right changes can be much more complicated. This gets to the central message of this book. Businesses and people often fail in improving their (and others) performance because identifying the right changes often gets lost in the various expectations and agendas of those involved, which leads them to make the wrong changes or only implement partial changes. I see and hear this happening more and more in businesses and am saddened by each instance, but what is really frustrating for Human Capital professionals such as myself, is when leaders waste company resources and cause unnecessary harm in the process.

To illustrate this point let me share a story from an average, publicly traded, company that wasted roughly 3 million dollars (and over 15,000 hours of lost production time) on a performance solution that not only failed, but was expected to fail by many of those that were involved in implementing it.

Every year, the sales group from this company conducted a conference where they would bring the sales leaders and the top sales members together for 4-5 days of training and meetings. Each year the conference would grow in attendance, but this particular year the company's financial struggles were so bad that the executives were debating whether the conference should be cancelled altogether. In response to this, the Chief Sales Officer pitched the need for the conference as a performance improvement opportunity. The conference was sold as a critical piece of the sales strategy, a necessary expenditure in order to mobilize the sales force, bring in more clients, and improve profits. Roughly 300 people attended the conference including myself, as an observer. The conference was held overseas, the center was beautiful, the food was delicious, there were lots of meetings and "training sessions," and everyone was busy the entire time. But, did this 3 million dollar conference bring improved profits? No. In fact, the company continued to lose clients and profits continued to decrease over the course of the next two years. Now I am not saying some good things didn't take place at the conference but it was the wrong solution to the performance gap it was attempting (or claiming) it was going to fill. As I said, I attended as an observer. I tried to find out what specific objectives they were going to achieve during the conference and how they were going to measure them, but they could not provide any. I interviewed several people in attendance before, during, and after, and was told by many that they thought it would be (or was) a waste of time and money. I attended many of the training sessions and discovered that while there were some very skilled sales people leading the sessions, many attendees were not listening to them. I even offered to provide and present an assessment report for future improvements but no one ever asked for it.

Now this may sound like an extreme example but as I said at the beginning, this took place in an average, publicly traded company. It happens a lot, and the worst cases tend not to be isolated instances. As a case in point, one would think that after wasting 3 million on an inappropriate and failed solution that they would learn a thing or two, but the following year the conference was back again. Even though the executive team had placed conditions on conducting future sales conferences, they were largely ignored. On the positive side, this time the conference was smaller and only cost 1 million but the result was the same. For some of the company leaders, this was seen as a performance improvement because they only spent 1 million this time, instead of 3, but why would anyone be OK with spending anything on a solution that has already proven to be a failure? I have heard it said that "insanity is doing the same thing over and over again, and expecting a different result." Sadly, there is too much insanity out there.

In this chapter we defined some basic terms and concepts, explained how they are connected, and demonstrated how people and business frequently waste their energy and resources by not understanding them and/ or making the wrong changes to fix them. In the next chapter we turn our attention to answering the most important question anyone seeking to improve performance must first answer, before they will ever have any real success.

3. HUMAN BEHAVIOR AND THE MOST IMPORTANT QUESTION

Over the centuries, people have theorized and debated thousands of questions regarding human behavior. However, their is one question anyone seeking to improve performance must first answer before they will ever have any real success. The question is this...*can people change?*

Perhaps you've heard the same internal (or external) voice that I struggled with for several years; "People don't change," "That's just who I am...I can't change," "A leopard can't change its spots." I would like to save you from wasting as much time as I have and assure you that the answer to that question is YES...PEOPLE CAN AND DO CHANGE! Unfortunately, what I say really doesn't matter unless you are convinced. You must believe it yourself or you will forever be plagued with failure in your efforts to change and improve performance. Simply put, if you do not think change is possible in a specific area, don't bother. You will not be successful. So, my purpose with the rest of this chapter is to thoroughly convince you that people can and do change.

In addition, I will seek to persuade you that there are very few things that cannot be changed. This is important because it is the source of the excuses we routinely fall back on and use so we do not even have to try. Yes, it may be hard. Yes, it may take longer than you want. Yes, the change may ultimately be out of your control. And, yes, you may decide the effort to change is not worth it. But, I have become increasingly convinced over time that there is very, very little that cannot be changed when it comes to behavior and performance. Once you start believing this for yourself, you will have taken the first step on the road to success, but trying to teach you how to change and improve performance when you don't believe it is possible, is like nailing Jello® to the wall. It just won't stick!

To start convincing you that people can and do change, or to further strengthen this belief if you already agree with it, I want to highlight some general principals of human behavior for you to consider. Of course, human behavior can be very complex and people can spend years studying and debating it. That is not my purpose or intent. For the purposes of this book, and more specifically to help convince you that people can and do change, we are only going to focus on two key aspects.

HUMANS ARE UNIQUELY SUITED FOR CHANGE

Whether you hold to a worldview that embraces the theory of intelligent design (that humans were created by an intelligent creator) or evolution (that humans are the product of millions or billions of years of natural and random biological adaptations) the first principle is that humans, above all known life forms, are unique in their ability to adapt and change. We call this process, learning. It's simple. It only takes one bee sting before you change your behavior around them. You learn. While other life forms are certainly capable of learning, none are as adept at the process as humans. This fact is supported by the scientific theory of Natural Selection or Survival of the Fittest; that those organisms that have adapted, or can adapt, to their surroundings or circumstances will survive, reproduce, and flourish. Those that have not, or cannot, will eventually diminish and/or disappear. Humans' ability to learn is unparalleled in the animal kingdom; it sets us apart and maintains our position at the top of the food chain. To demonstrate this for you I will share three examples. First, let's consider the examples of the monkey trap and the first lion encounter.

Twenty years ago I read an article about how natives in Africa and the Pacific Islands would go about trapping monkeys alive. I was a bit skeptical at first but discovered it was true and later witnessed it through some video footage. Natives will drill a hole in coconut or in a termite mound, put some food into the hole and walk away. Monkeys will see or smell the food, stick their hand in the hole, and grab the food. Once they do this, their hand (now in the form of a fist) becomes too big to pull it out of the hole.

While the monkey frantically tries to get the food out, the trapper can simply walk up to the monkey and place a leash around its neck. Believe it or not, the monkey will not let go of the food to run away. Now we as humans we would simply let go of the food, withdraw our hand, and run. So what is different about us? Well, I am going to assume that you won't dispute the fact that the brain functioning and mental ability of humans far exceed that of all other animals, but there is another key reason we as humans are unique in our ability to adapt and change; our ability to communicate. Of course it is true that all animals communicate with each other. Birds chirp, dogs bark, and whales sing, but they can't say, "Hey, let go of the food in your hand and you will be able to get away." Our ability to communicate not only allows us to share details of what we learn today, but we can pass on the details of what we, and others, have learned from the past. This leads us to the example of the first lion encounter.

Have you ever considered the first time mankind encountered a lion? Of course, no one really knows what happened but imagine no one had ever seen or heard of a lion. One day a man is walking through the jungle and sees a beautiful flower. He is captivated by it. At the same time a lion comes walking by. Never having seen one, and having no reason to be concerned, his attention continues to be consumed by the flower and the lion makes an easy meal of him. So how did we ever overcome this situation? Why is it that this behavior doesn't continue? Simple, we learned that lions are dangerous. We changed our behavior. At some point in history, someone must have experienced a situation like this and was lucky enough to survive and tell someone else. Or maybe someone saw it happen to someone else and shared the information with others. Or maybe they saw how some other large animal killed someone. In any case, they learned that lions are dangerous and then shared that information with others. At some point in your life this same information has been shared with you, perhaps through books, videos, TV, or word of mouth, and I am willing to bet that if you are ever walking through the jungle and see a beautiful flower, you will stop looking at it the second you see or hear a lion nearby.

A more historical example that illustrates how human communication skills magnify our ability to adapt and change more than any other life form, is that of the American pilgrims. Most Americans probably know this story. When the Pilgrims landed at Plymouth Rock, Mass. in 1620 and began to settle in the area, they were ill suited to survive the harsh winter conditions they encountered. Many got sick and by the end of the winter, half of the colony died. Yet only a year later things were very different. Not only did they survive the but they began to flourish and over the course of the next 70 years they grew to a colony of over 7,000 members. So, how did they do this? They learned! They changed! And, they were aided in this process through the ability to communicate.

The Native American Indians who had lived in the region for centuries were well suited and used to surviving in such conditions and it was by befriending them that the Pilgrims learned what and how they needed to change in order to survive. Now since they did not speak the local natives language, the process of befriending and learning from them would likely have taken several years and the colony may have ended, but two of the natives were able to speak English. This made the process significantly easier. Through these two ambassadors, the Pilgrims were able to learn and adapt to their new environment more quickly. The following year, the Pilgrims had experienced a successful harvest and held a 3 day feast to thank God for His provision to them and to honor the natives that had helped them so much. Thus was born what most consider to be the first American "Thanksgiving."

YOU DO WHAT YOU THINK

The second principle of human behavior you should consider as you answer the question of whether people can and do change, is that our behaviors and emotions are predominantly determined by what we think or know (a.k.a. what we have learned). Let me illustrate this with something everyone can relate to. At some point in your life you learned that touching fire is dangerous and will cause pain. As previously discussed, you may learn this through personal experience or perhaps you learned it through someone telling you. Either way, what you think or know about fire keeps you from touching it, a behavior, and produces fear, an emotion, when confronted with the prospect of doing so.

This principle of doing what we think affects almost every behavior or emotion we express. What makes this complicated is that we think and know a lot of things, and they all interact with each other based on the situations we encounter. Let me explain this by continuing with the fire example. Based on what we have learned about fire (what we think or know), we would all avoid running into a burning building. Now let's insert a crying, helpless baby into the equation. Would that change your behavior? Would it change your emotions? What if you had a fire-retardant suit and oxygen tank at your disposal? Would that change your behavior? Would it change your emotions? While we started with the basic premise that fire is dangerous, to be avoided, and something to be feared, what we think and know about the situation can be overridden and cause us to behave and feel differently.

Here is another example that may illustrate the point for you. When Americans look at the following number, 911, we will see one of two things; the phone number we use to report an emergency situation, or the date that Islamic terrorists crashed two planes into the World Trade Center in New York. Prior to September 11, 2001, when an American looked at this number only one answer would have been given for its meaning, but on that day something terrible happened. What we think and know changed and now our response to the number has been altered. For some, we still see the emergency number. For others, this number now gives rise to a very different set of thoughts, emotions, and even actions. What we think and know drives what we do.

There Is Little That Cannot Be Changed

Now that you have a clear understanding of these basic principles regarding human behavior and how they can impact or determine performance, we can get to the job of determining where you personally stand on the question of…do people change? As I said before, I know people can and do change. Not only do they change but there are very few things that cannot be changed, and those things are becoming fewer and fewer as time goes by. Now, if you are like everyone else I have interviewed, your mind is already trying to think of things that cannot be changed. That's good! Let's think that way together for a bit, but keep in mind that we are specifically talking about changing behavior and performance. Below are three broad categories that people I have interviewed initially tell me cannot be changed. My goal here is to present you with the same challenges I have posed to them to change their initial thinking and thereby change their behavior…and potentially yours too.

You Can't Change Your Past

The first category that people say cannot be changed is… the past. Until we have the ability to travel back in time, it is true that you cannot really change your past. However, people effectively change their past every day. They change their names. They change who their parents are. They cover-up and remove records of indiscretions they may have previously committed. Some have even falsified their death and created entirely new identities/pasts for themselves. In all of these cases, no one has "truly" changed their past but let's be honest with ourselves, from a performance or behavioral perspective, success is typically based on the outcome, not the empirical facts. Often, these outcomes are for the benefit of, or to influence, others. In this regard, you could argue that these people have been successful in changing their past. For example, I look, and have always considered myself to be of Caucasian ethnicity. However, after a few years of working in the business world, I discovered that a person's chance of being hired can be improved if they are found to be part of a "diverse" ethnic group. Since then, when applying for jobs with a company, I will sometimes check the box indicating that I am of Hispanic ethnicity. Now, I can legally do this because I technically am Hispanic. My father is of Spanish decent and was born in Lima, Peru. Even though people do not perceive me as being Hispanic, I can change this aspect of my past to improve the performance I desire or need. True, I have not really changed my past, but I know this has been effective and has helped me with getting interviews. In this regard I would argue that I have been successful in changing my past, or the perception of it.

You Can't Change Your Biological Makeup

Another category that people say cannot be changed is… their biological makeup. Really? Can you change your hair? Can you change your eye color? Can you change your weight? Your height? The color of your skin? The answer to all these is, yes, and unlike the example of changing your past, many of these can be made permanent. Let me explain. You can change your hair by cutting it, styling it, coloring it, or removing it altogether. You can change your eyes by wearing colored or decorative contact lenses. You can change your height by putting lifts in your shoes. While all of these changes are relatively simple to achieve and maintain in our modern society, they are temporary. Now let's take this a step further. One way you can change your weight is by eating less and exercising more, but you can also change it by liposuction or surgically decreasing the size of your stomach. Unlike eating less or exercising, where your fat cells simply shrink but never disappear, liposuction permanently removes the fat cells. It is a real and permanent change. You can also change your height permanently. Rather than putting lifts inside your shoes each morning, you can insert lifts directly into your legs by having bone extensions. That's right, a surgeon can actually cut you open and graft additional bone in your femur to make you taller. You can also change the color of your skin. As an example of this, I would simply draw your attention to the former King of Pop, Michael Jackson, or people that frequent tanning salons.

Now putting lifts in your shoes, eating less, and visiting a tanning salon are simple and affordable enough for most people. However, the effort and cost associated with plastic surgery, liposuction, or bone extensions is considerably more costly. So, while I have demonstrated that it is possible to change your biological makeup, some of these changes (the more permanent and costly ones) may also be less accessible. Not because they are not possible, but because many of us simply lack the resources to make them happen.

As you consider the possibility of changes in this category, you should also consider that many of the solutions discussed did not even exist until a few decades ago. This is what I meant in my earlier statement that, "there are very few things that cannot be changed, and those things are becoming fewer and fewer as time goes by." As medical technology and practices evolve, more and more characteristics, conditions, and changes to the human body have moved from the realm of science fiction to science fact. One of the frontiers of this shift is the science of Genetic Engineering and Gene Therapy. While still in their infancy, their whole focus is to introduce permanent change at the cellular level. Having already experienced great success in the fields of agriculture and pharmacology, human applications in genetics are still largely experimental. Regardless, trials have been shown to be successful in removing some hereditary mutations such as blindness and maternal diabetes, as well as treating certain immunodeficiency diseases. There is still a long way to go but the expectation is that one day we will be able to make changes to genes that controls skin color, height, strength, and maybe even intelligence.

Regardless of the future's potential, it is possible today to change your biological makeup, and while some changes may be beyond our ability to afford, not worth the side effects, or still firmly rooted in the realm of science fiction, time will make more of them possible and more accessible.

You Can't Change Your Personality

The last category that people tend to say cannot be changed is…their personality. This may be the hardest category to challenge because it largely depends on how you define, and what you believe about, personalities. Does God create a unique personality within you as you are being knitted together in your mother's womb? Is it the result of your genetic make-up? Is it simply an expression of your environment and upbringing? Volumes of material have been written on the formation of the human personality but again, my purpose is not to debate definitions, rather to convince you that people's personalities can and do change. To this end, let's take a basic definition of personality which clearly aligns with what we have previously discussed. According to Merriam-Webster[1], Personality is:

"The complex of characteristics that distinguishes an individual or a nation or group; especially: the totality of an individual's behavioral and emotional characteristics."

In other words, you are an onion. That's right, an onion. Take an outer peel off an onion and what do you have? The answer is…an onion. Peel more of the skins off the onion and what do you have? An onion. Keep going until you have nothing left and up until that point, you still have an onion. The fact is, an onion is nothing more than a collection of skins. Your personality is the collection of your onionskins. You are, your personality is, the result of what you do and how you feel. Since we have already demonstrated how what we think can change what we do and how we feel, it should be clear that we can change our personality. We also discussed how we can also change what others think of us, and therefore how they feel and behave toward us. As such, we change others perception of our personality. What we think, how we feel, what we do, and even how we look are all able to be changed to various degrees and it is for these reasons that I say, there is very little that cannot be changed.

People That Have Changed

Based on what has been presented so far, my hope is that I have at least begun to convince you that change is possible. To help drive this idea home, let's look at this from another perspective. Let's look at a few examples of people that have succeeded in changing the very things that we've discussed and that most of those interviewed thought could not be changed.

We have already mentioned Michael Jackson as an example of someone who succeeded in changing their physical appearance (in a very drastic way). These types of physical changes have become so common over the last few decades that I do not see providing more examples as being all that useful. What is more useful, is to provide examples of people that have changed their past and their personality.

Let's first look at Marion Morrison. Marion was an average guy. Got good grades, played football, received an athletic scholarship and went to

---

1   Merriam-Webster. February 12, 2013. <http://www.merriam-webster.com/>

college at the University of Southern California as a pre-law student, but later had to drop out because of an injury. What is interesting about Marion is that most people know who he is but almost no one knows him as Marion or remembers what he did for the first 22 years of his life. Why? Because he changed his name and his behavior (his profession). In 1930, he stopped pursuing law and developed an acting career that defined the rest of his life, and even after his death. The name we all know him by is John Wayne.

Now let's consider another example. Have you ever heard of John Johnson? In the early 1980s, John Johnson was living in Austin, Texas. He purchased a hot dog and fajita cart and began to develop a thriving business. 10 years later, in 1991, he ran for mayor of Austin and made an astonishing announcement. Prior to 1980, his name was John Patrick Tully, a convicted murderer and hit man for the Campisi crime family of Newark, New Jersey. John was a participant in the U.S. Witness Protection Program and had succeeded in changing his past (or having it changed for himself) so thoroughly that only a few in Austin's law enforcement community knew any different.

John is not the only person to participate in the Witness Protection Program and have their entire past rewritten. Of course, the whole purpose of the program it to keep these witnesses unknown. It is only, like John, those who spilled the beans, or got kicked out of the program, that we know anything about. There may be hundreds of others witnesses still out there, but thanks to John we have a clear example that it is possible to successfully change your past.

In addition to these examples of people that have changed their past, there are others that have succeeded in changing their personality. For example, millions of people struggle with, and succeed at overcoming, substance addictions. If you know anyone in this category you should already be well aware that this is a personality (behaviors and emotions) and that people can and do change it. If however you do not know of anyone, let me introduce you to one, American author Stephen King. Stephen has written several bestselling books, many of which have been turned into major motion pictures. These include such best sellers as; *Carrie, The Shining, The Stand, Christine, The Shawshank Redemption* and *The Green Mile*. Over time, Stephen increasingly struggled with alcoholism and drug abuse. In the late 1980s his addiction became so extreme his wife and children staged an intervention. Since then, he has succeeded in remaining sober. How did he make this change? According to his own comments, a large part involved changing how he thinks, how he feels, and what he does.

One example of this is visible in an article he wrote in 2007. He writes the following:

> "…if my own career as a drunk both active and sober has convinced me of anything, it's convinced me of this: addictive personalities do not prosper on their own. Without unvarnished, tough-love truth-telling from their own kind—the voices that say, 'You're lying about that, Freckles'—the addict has a tendency to fall back into his old ways."[1]

Substance addiction is an incredibly difficult performance/behavior to change, and Stephen's is just one of a million examples that show how such a difficult change can be sustained over time.

Saul of Tarsus is another great example of a changed personality. His thinking, behavior, and emotions were so radically changed it demonstrates one of the most dramatic, historically documented, examples of change in a human's life that I can think of. For those who do not know, Saul of Tarsus, was born sometime around 1 AD. He was a Jewish Rabbi, a teacher of the law, and in most respects, an aristocrat. Though Jewish, he was also a Roman citizen. The story of his changed personality can be found in the Bible but rather than me explaining, I'll let him do it himself.

> **Before:**
>
> "As the Jews are well aware, I was given a thorough Jewish training from my earliest childhood in Tarsus and later at Jerusalem, and I lived accordingly. If they would admit it, they know that I have always been the strictest of Pharisees when it comes to obedience to Jewish laws and customs…I used to believe that I ought to do many horrible things to the followers of Jesus of Nazareth. I imprisoned many of the saints in Jerusalem, as authorized by the High Priests; and when they were condemned to death, I cast my vote against them. I used torture to try to make Christians everywhere curse Christ. I was so violently opposed to them that I even hounded them in distant cities in foreign lands." [2]
>
> "Yet if anyone ever had reason to hope that he could save

---

1   King, Stephen. "Frey's Lies." Entertainment Weekly. February 1, 2007. Web. January 1, 2013. <http:// www.ew.com/ew/article/0,,1155752,00.html>

2   Acts 26:4-5, 9-11 The Living Bible

himself, it would be I. If others could be saved by what they are, certainly I could! For I went through the Jewish initiation ceremony when I was eight days old, having been born into a pure-blooded Jewish home that was a branch of the old original Benjamin family. So I was a real Jew if there ever was one! What's more, I was a member of the Pharisees who demand the strictest obedience to every Jewish law and custom. And sincere? Yes, so much so that I greatly persecuted the Church; and I tried to obey every Jewish rule and regulation right down to the very last point." [1]

After:
"But all these things that I once thought very worthwhile—now I've thrown them all away so that I can put my trust and hope in Christ alone. Yes, everything else is worthless when compared with the priceless gain of knowing Christ Jesus my Lord. I have put aside all else, counting it worth less than nothing, in order that I can have Christ." [2]

"And so, O King Agrippa, I was not disobedient to that vision from heaven! I preached [about Jesus] first to those in Damascus, then in Jerusalem and through Judea, and also to the Gentiles that all must forsake their sins and turn to God—and prove their repentance by doing good deeds. The Jews arrested me in the Temple for preaching this and tried to kill me, but God protected me so that I am still alive today to tell these facts to everyone, both great and small." [3]

As you have read, Saul's encounter with Jesus forever changed him, from that day until his death some 27 years later, around 60AD. He became a different man. Because of his changed personality, Saul, also known as the Apostle Paul, became one of the most influential men in world history. However, my point here is not to preach a sermon on how God can change a person's life, or even how He changed Saul's life. My point is simply to

---

1   Philippians 3:4-6 The Living Bible
2   Philippians 3:7-8 The Living Bible
3   Acts 26:19-20 The Living Bible

demonstrate that personality (what you think, how you feel, what you do, and how others perceive you) can change.

Finally, I have one more example of someone who has changed…me. I am only including myself to provide a common, everyday, "nothing special about me," perspective. Also, as I noted earlier, I'm a "show me the proof" kind of guy, so it would be remiss of me not to share a little about my own experiments in change and performance improvement.

As I previously shared, I have struggled with the question of whether change is really possible for much of my life. It was often just easier to buy into the line that there are "some things that you just can't change." But, with the knowledge I had gained in school, and my experience working as a minister and corporate trainer, I began to more purposely apply, modify and test various principles of performance improvement in my own life. Slowly, and over several years, I discovered that I could not only change things that had struggled with for years, but that those changes could become permanent and lasting parts of my life. At first, I purposefully began changing some simple behaviors like:

- Regularly flossing my teeth everyday instead of only doing it a few days before a dentist appointment.
- Wiping off the glass shower door after every shower rather than leaving it for my wife to do or allowing water spots to form.

As these simple tests proved to be successful, I began to experiment with some bigger changes like losing weight and keeping it off. So far, the majority of the changes I have made have stuck. I am flossing every day, wiping off the glass shower door, and have maintained a weight loss of 30 pounds. Interestingly, some behaviors I changed, as far back as 2001, have become so thoroughly ingrained that they have proven even more challenging to change back. And if you are curious, yes…there are changes I have failed to make. But, in all of these situations I know exactly why I have failed and what is required to change them. I have discovered that there are only three causes for all performance gaps (Hills, Skills, and Wills). I have also learned how to identify them and use that information to develop and implement solutions that actually work. Now it is time for you to do the same!

To wrap up this chapter, I explained that what you think defines how you behave and how you behave against expectations defines your performance. Also, people can and do change. In fact, there are fewer and fewer things that cannot be changed. It may take you some more time to absorb these ideas and I would encourage you to do so. In fact, I challenge you to try and think of one thing that cannot be changed as it relates to your (or others) performance/behavior. Make an effort to poke a hole in what I have shared, but remember this…until you believe people can and do change, you are unlikely to succeed or improve performance.

4. HILLS, SKILLS, AND WILLS

Why do so many of the efforts by individuals, companies and governments to improve performance fail? The answer begins with three words; Hills, Skills, and Wills. I can't even begin to tell you how much money, time, and energy is spent on failed and misguided efforts to improve performance simply because people did not know or pay attention to these three little words. Of course, this is where Performance Improvement practitioners like me come in. We make our living by helping business leaders avoid and correct these failures. We teach them how to do this for themselves and we tell them when they aren't paying enough attention to them. So how do we do this and, more importantly, how can you?

First, you need to realize that every performance gap experienced by an individual or organization comes from one, or some combination, of three primary causes…Hills, Skills, and Wills. There are no exceptions to this, none! Being able to remember these three causes is the first and most critical step to resolving performance gaps. If you can memorize these three words, you can answer the "WHY" behind every performance issue that humanity has ever faced. Why is there political unrest in the Middle East? Hills, Skills, and Wills. Why are your company sales decreasing? Hills, Skills, and Wills. Why can't you lose weight? Hills, Skills, and Wills.

Of course there is more to resolving performance gaps than memorizing these three words, but you need to understand what they are. You need to be able to recognize them. You need to understand why they are so important and why people so often fail to see or correct them. Finally, you need to be able to correctly identify which are at the root of your performance gaps so that you can develop a targeted solution to resolve them.

Mastery of these skills will exponentially increase your chances of success in improving performance. However, we need to start slow and build this mastery one step at a time, so let's start by individually explaining each of the three causes in more detail. Along with these explanations, I will provide you some examples from both a business and individual perspective. These examples will each start in an overly simplistic manner so you can easily grasp the concepts. As you progress the examples will become more realistic, and in later chapters, more complex. Finally, to help you build your confidence, you will also be given the opportunity to practice identifying them for yourself.

Hills

We begin with Hills. As most of you are aware, a hill is a large mound of earth. It is an physical obstacle that typically separates people or places. It requires us to go around it, under it, though it, or over it, in order to get to our desired destination.

In the case of a performance gap, Hills are the same. They are obstacles (typically physical) that block us, and others, from doing what is needed or expected, from getting to our destination.

For simplicity's sake, let's say a salesperson is expected to make a certain number of sales every day but their phone keeps dropping calls or maybe they don't have a phone at all. This is a physical obstacle that will most certainly block them from meeting the expected performance. Likewise, we could take an individual who is constantly late to events because his or her car continually breaks down. The lack of a reliable form of transportation is a physical obstacle to the expected performance of being on time to events. Both of these performance gaps would be categorized as Hill gaps, because they are due to physical obstacles that block the performers from being able to do what is needed, desired, or expected.

Can you begin to think of Hill gaps that you regularly encounter in your life, or others encounter in their lives? How about a triathlete that has a pulled hamstring? How about a drunk driver trying to pass a sobriety test?

How about a soldier that needs to quickly get to the other side of a live mine field? Each of these has an unreached performance expectation that is being caused by some physical obstacle.

One of the most common Hill gaps that companies across the world are routinely engaged in resolving, has to do with technology. In fact, I will bet you that at this very minute, almost every major corporation in the world is currently involved in updating, replacing, or consolidating their technologies. Why? Since the invention of the wheel, technology has allowed us to do things faster, simpler, and sometimes better. However, at other times, technology becomes an obstacle (a Hill) to improving performance. Many companies are consolidating computer hardware and software with the expectation that it will allow their employees to work faster and do more than they were previously able. Some companies systems are simply outdated and can no longer handle the workload they once could. In other cases, as we have probably all experienced, our technology is at risk of being hacked, infected, or otherwise compromised. Do you remember Y2K, also known as the Millennium Bug? This is one of my favorite Hill examples for several reasons, but particularly because of its widespread impact.

In 1999, the world was in a bit of a panic that caused most companies and organizations to invest significant sums of money to update their computer systems before January 1, 2000. Why? Because computer programmers had pretty much standardized the practice of having their software shorten all dates in order to save space and processing time. As such, when a computer was presented with a date of 80 or 10, it presumed the date to be 1980 or 1910. Unfortunately, as we approached the year 2000, it became apparent that computers would now needed to be able to distinguish between 1910 and 2010 or 1980 and 2080. As a result of this programming oversight, end of the world scenarios began to emerge as awareness of the issue grew. Since more and more things were being controlled by computers, people began to fear that they would simply stop working on January 1st. The stock market would crash, planes would start falling from the skies, missile systems would malfunction, and company computers would go haywire. In total, an estimated 100 to 600 billion dollars was spent upgrading systems before January 1st to ensure the end of the world did not happen. In short, a physical obstacle, the way computers interpreted dates, had to be resolved in order to maintain performance and avert the coming apocalypse.

SKILLS

Now let's look at Skills. Riding a bike is a skill. Reading is a skill. Removing someone's appendix or gall bladder is a skill. Unlike Hill gaps, Skill gaps are mental, not physical, obstacles.

Skill gaps come from a lack of "know how." The person or group simply does not know, or know how to_____. Using the previous examples, perhaps our fictitious salesperson owns the best phone money can buy, but does not know how to use it. Or maybe they know how to use the phone but they don't know anything about the products or services they are expected to sell. In either case, they do not know how, or have the necessary skills, to meet the performance and will therefore continue to fall short. Likewise, the individual who is expected or looking to be on time more consistently could purchase a more reliable car, but they will continue to be late if they do not know how to drive it, or know the directions to get to the event. Both of these performance gaps would be categorized as Skill gaps, because the performers do not know how to do what is needed, desired, or expected.

Like we did with Hills, consider your own experience. How have Skill gaps limited your and/or others ability to perform as desired or expected? Have you ever received a poor or failing grade on a test because you didn't know the correct answers to the questions? Have you ever gotten a parking ticket because you didn't know that parking wasn't allowed on Tuesdays between 7:00 and 8:30am? Have you ever begun a new job and been less than effective because you didn't know how to submit an expense report, order business cards, change your computer password, or what people were talking about when they asked for a P&L, RFP, RFI, or SOP? Did you even know where to go or who to ask in order to get answers to these and other questions? These are all Skill gaps, and while some may not pose a major performance issue in themselves, the more of them a person has and the more people that experience them, the more they will begin to have a significant effect. In some cases, even being unaware of a single piece of information can have a huge effect. For instance, not realizing that something as simple as asking someone where they were born during an interview could be a violation of the U.S. Equal Employment Opportunities Act and not only cost you your job but cost your company millions of dollars in an employment lawsuit.

In the U.S. alone, companies spent about 160 billion dollars in 2011 trying to make sure their employees knew what they needed to know. Unfortunately, the pressure for businesses to perform continues to increase, as does the pressure on the people working in those businesses, so things can and do slip through the cracks. As such, if a performance is not being met and you are certain there are no physical obstacles causing the gap, you may be experiencing a Skill gap.

WILLS

Finally, we come to the third cause of performance gaps, Wills. Interestingly, Wills are the primary cause of most performance gaps as experienced by both organizations and individuals. Simply put, a Will gap is any gap in performance that occurs when a person decides that the effort required to meet the desired expectation, "is just not worth it."

Now we have all probably encountered situations where this gap is plainly evident. Perhaps some immediately come to your mind. Some examples that others have shared with me, or that I have experienced myself, include the teenage store clerk that is talking to his or her friends on the phone and gives you the "stink eye" when you dare to ask them for help. There's the tenured college professor that uses pre- recorded audio of his lectures rather than coming to class. There's also the government worker that seem incapable of answering anyone's questions except to tell them that they need to fill out and submit yet another form. In each of these situations, it feels as though the person just doesn't care. They don't care about you, they don't care about doing their job well and, they don't care about whatever it is that they should be caring about. BE CAREFUL! Just because it looks or feels like they don't care doesn't mean it's true. More importantly, remember that "not caring" isn't the definition of a Will gap. A Will gap occurs when a person decides that the effort required to meet the desired expectation, "is just not worth it." Sometime people really do care, but they simply find greater worth in doing something else.

For instance, let's go back and look at the fictitious salesperson example we used when explaining Hills and Skills. Perhaps the salesperson owns the best phone in the world (Hill gap resolved), they know how to use it, know everything about the products they have to sell, and have been the most successful salesperson in the company for several years (Skill gaps resolved). Now let's say the company comes under new management. The new management decides that salespeople will no longer be paid extra for each sale they make over their quota. Instead, all salespeople will make the same salary regardless of whether they sell five widgets, or one million. Chances are, the salesperson's will to sell more than their quota will decrease because there is no longer as much value in doing so. It is just not worth it! Likewise, in our other fictitious example of the late party-goer, an individual may buy a new car, learn how to drive it, and have the correct directions, but they will continue to be late to events if the satisfaction they get from arriving last is more worthwhile to them than being on time. In both of these cases, the performance gaps would be categorized as Will gaps because the performers simply did not find the expected or desired performance to be as worthwhile as doing something else (or doing nothing at all).

One performance issue that organizations routinely struggle with, and that is predominantly caused by a Will gap, is employee retention. When an employee permanently leaves an organization, it not only loses the production value of that employee, but they lose the investment they put in training that employee. They can also incur additional costs to find and retrain a new employee. They may even lose some of their clients, such as when a salesperson leaves, gets hired by a competitor, and takes his knowledge and clients with him. So why do people leave organizations? There is a well-known saying in the Human Resource community that people don't leave companies, they leave managers. Of course this is not always true, however, more frequently than not, the reason people leave companies is because they don't like those they are working for or with. An employee's dislike for, or frustration with, a coworker, manager, or leader can grow to the point where the worth they had from having that job is overshadowed by the worth of not having to deal with them anymore. I have seen this scenario play out repeatedly in families, churches, small businesses, and large corporations. To make matters worse, when someone leaves an organization it is typically just the final act. In nearly every case, performance begins to erode in direct relation to the loss of those things the person defines as "worthwhile." Typically this happens over an extended period of time. The longer it is left unresolved and the more it happens, the greater the decrease in performance. In some cases, it can become so toxic that people actually begin to purposely sabotage efforts of the organization as a way of retaliating for their losses. This is a sad situation on multiple levels. It's sad because many people remain in jobs where the only worth remaining is the paycheck, and even that is dwindling. It is also sad because of the impact it has on the organization. This single Will gap costs companies millions of dollars every year in outcomes like decreased production quality or volumes, and litigation expenses.

The good news is, it doesn't have to be this way. By being aware and carefully paying attention to what people deem worthwhile, you can not only improve their performance but begin to attract the most qualified people to your organization.

So there you have it. The three primary causes that prevent people from performing as expected are:

1. Hills: obstacles (typically physical) that block us from doing what is needed or expected
2. Skills: not knowing what or how to do what is needed or expected
3. Wills: deciding that the effort required to meet the need or expectation is just not worth it.

On the next page are five fictitious scenarios involving performance gaps. Before continuing, take a minute to review each scenario and see if you can identify what the most likely cause is for the gap between what they want and where they are. The answers can be found at the end of the chapter.

1. Tim won two free tickets for an exclusive seven day cruise in the Bahamas. He wants to go but is considering selling the ticket to his friends because he's deathly afraid of the ocean.
2. Philip has always loved planes. He has been saving his money for the last four years so he can become a pilot. Finally having saved enough, he went down to the local airfield and signed up for an all-inclusive flight training program.
3. Sally has wanted to be a lawyer since she was 10-years-old. In pursuing her goal, she just graduated at the top of her class at Yale Law School. She has a job offer from a firm but it is dependent on her passing the bar exam.
4. Jerry wants a promotion. He has been overlooked by the company leadership because he is perceived as a push-over. He has good ideas and knows how to make a strong business case but is afraid to voice or defend his ideas in meetings because his previous employer would reprimand him every time he did.
5. Ellen is deaf but is determined to learn how to play the piano.

Why Is This Important?

So now that we have discussed what Hills, Skills, and Wills are, let's briefly talk about the importance that understanding and remembering them can bring when seeking to improve performance. There are hundreds of reasons why improving performance is important. Below is a short list of some of the most common benefits associated with improving performance:

- Increased productivity
- Greater financial success
- Career advancement
- Increased work and/or personal satisfaction
- Recognition from others
- Greater security

This list seem pretty obvious. Every one of us wants to experience some or all of these benefits at some point in our lives, but sometimes the importance of improving performance is not defined by the benefits we receive as much as it is by the ramifications of not improving performance.

No one likes to fail! No one wants to fail! Failure to improve performance has a price, and sometimes that price can be great. The price can be emotional, such as hurt feelings, frustration, or disappointment. The price can be physical, such as a broken leg or a heart attack. Quite often, the price is financial, such as wasted investments, decreased profits or maybe bankruptcy. As bad as these ramifications for failing to improve performance are, or can be, there is one that is often overlooked. Even worse than the emotional, physical, and financial price, failure to improve performance means that the problem or gap is still there. Suffering a heart attack because you eat too much fatty foods is bad enough, but if you don't change your eating habit, what do you think is going to happen? Similarly, if employees continue to leave your company because their manager is a jerk, what do you think will happen by ignoring that manager's behavior?

The importance of understanding the framework of Hills, Skills, and Wills is that it can significantly help you to improve performance, and avoid or correct failed attempts, by making it easier to identify and focuses your attention on the root causes behind performance gaps. In turn, this will make the solution you develop more targeted and provide a way to assess the appropriateness of those solutions.

WHY DO WE FAIL?

Even those that understand what Hills, Skills, and Wills are, and realize the importance of improving their performance, often fail in their efforts. So, let's look at the reasons why this happens. The reasons why people and organizations fail so often (even if they are aware of the three main causes) is that they/we misdiagnose the cause of the gap, or ignore it. As a result, we end up missing or solving the wrong problems. For example, we may think a problem is caused by a Hill when it's actually caused by a Will or Skill. In some cases, people may even know the problem is being caused by a Will gap but simply chose to ignore it, and convince themselves (or others) that the cause is a Hill. Consider this. Have you (or someone you know) ever purchased an expensive piece of exercise equipment thinking it will solve your weight problem, only to find a month later it is collecting dust in the garage and that you have actually gained a few pounds since then? Have you (or someone you know) ever purchased a health club membership with the same mindset, only to find you have been paying your dues for months but haven't stepped foot in the building after the first two weeks you purchased the membership? We mistakenly believe, or convince ourselves, that not having the equipment or membership (a Hill gap) is the root cause of the problem. But what is the more likely cause? The health club industry knows the answer to that question, and their business thrives on it.

The fitness club industry knows that many people have an intense desire to be healthier but are often unwilling to invest the time and energy to actually exercise (a Will gap). They know that they can sell more memberships to more people than their clubs can accommodate, because they know that a large number of them will stop coming shortly after they purchase the membership. If you don't believe me, check out the statistics. An April 2012 report[1] from the health club industry determined that 67% of club memberships go unused.

So why is identifying the correct cause of this performance gap so difficult and why do people sometimes ignore it? This is a bit of a trick question. Remember I already told you at the beginning of this chapter that every performance gap experienced by an individual or organization comes from of one, or some combination, of three primary causes…Hills, Skills, and Wills. There are no exceptions to this, none!

Misdiagnosing or ignoring the true cause of a performance gap is simply another performance gap. There is either some obstacle keeping them from identifying the correct gap (Hill), they do not know how to identify the correct gap (Skill), or identifying the correct gap is just not worth it (Will). I know this may be starting to sound complicated but it is important to understanding that there is often more than one Hill, Skill, and Will, involved in both the cause and continued failures to resolve performance gaps. Taking this into account, a company may be losing clients because:

- They don't have enough product to meet the needs (a Hill gap)
- Their salespeople don't know how to sell (a Skills gap)

In addition, the owner of the company may misdiagnose the situation and think the reason they are losing clients is:

- His salespeople are simply lazy (a misdiagnosed Will gap)

Let's further look at this phenomena using our health club membership example. The table on the next page shows two people experiencing the same performance gap. In both cases they incorrectly identify the lack of a health club membership as the cause, but notice that there is only one actual cause for the first person while the second has three actual causes. Also notice

---

1   Statistics Brain. February 28, 2013. <http://www.statisticbrain.com/gym-membership-statistics>.

46

how there can be one or more factors that cause them to misdiagnose the actual cause.

	Person 1	Person 2
Gap	• A failure to lose weight or to get in shape	• A failure to lose weight or to get in shape
Misdiagnosed Cause	• Lack of a club membership (a Hill gap)	• Lack of a club membership (a Hill gap)
Actual Cause(s)	• Unwilling to invest the time and energy to actually exercise (a Will gap)	• Unwilling to invest the time and energy to actually exercise (a Will gap) • Does not know what kinds of exercise to do or how to do them (a Skill gap) • Has a hormonal condition that restricts weight loss and makes them tired all the time (a Hill gap)
Cause(s) of Misdiagnosis	• Unwillingness to admit personal responsibility for lack of weight loss (a Will gap)	• Peer pressure from friends to join the club with them (a Will gap) • Unaware that they could lose weight and get in shape without club equipment (a Skill gap) • Unable to afford medication to treat medical condition (a Hill gap)

In life, the number of gaps contributing to a failure in performance, or the failure in its improvement, can be great or small. However, regardless of how many gaps may exist, they are all caused by the same three things; Hills, Skills, and Wills. There are no exceptions to this, none!

In the next chapter, we will explore two true stories that demonstrate how the lessons learned in this chapter are played out in the real lives of people and organizations. We'll see how gaps are caused by Hills, Skills, and Wills.

We'll see and define the importance of the failures that were experienced in each story. And, we'll see how people misdiagnose and/or simply ignore the causes because of the same three causes; Hills, Skills, and Wills.

ANSWER TO QUESTIONS ON PAGE 44

1. Will Gap: The worth he sees in going on the vacation is being challenged by the worth he see in not drowning at sea.

2. Skill Gap: He sees it as a worth his effort and has the money to acquire all the resources needed. The only thing lacking is what he will learn in the flight training program.

3. Hill Gap: She has proven she has the knowledge to pass the bar exam, is able to take tests, and sees great worth is doing so, until she actually takes the test she won't get the job.

4. Will Gap: While it is possible the leadership team is incorrect in their assessment of the manager, he has decided to the effort to defend his ideas is not worth the effort.

5. Hill and Skill Gaps: Her lack of hearing is a physical obstacle and she does not know how to play the piano yet

5. TRUE STORIES

At this point in our journey we have seen how all performance gaps are caused by Hills, Skills, and Wills. We have discussed the importance that our failure to improve performance can have. We have shown how people can misdiagnose and/or simply ignore the true causes of the gap because of other Hills, Skills, and Wills. In this chapter, I will share two true stories that demonstrate these very lessons. Neither of these stories is an extreme case, although those do exist. I believe sharing accounts that are fairly average will make them easier to relate to. The first story highlights the performance of an individual while the second focuses on performance within a business.

MY FRIEND'S NEW CAR

When I was in my 20's, I had a friend who was full of energy, very outgoing, very disorganized, and most importantly, habitually late to every event or meeting he was invited to. Those of us that knew him understood and eventually just accepted this about him but his parents were continually frustrated, and sometimes embarrassed, by his inability to be on time. One day, I was pulling into the house my friend and I were renting and saw a brand new car sitting in the driveway. I knew he had been talking about wanting a new car but I also knew he could not afford one. As it turns out, he had told his parents that his car kept breaking down and he was having trouble getting to his job on time. He also mentioned to them that he was hoping to get a new car when he could afford it. As he framed it, the old car was the obstacle (a Hill gap) and the solution to it was the new car in the driveway. Now we made good use of the new car (i.e. road trips) but do you think it changed his performance in any way? Of course not! This was not a Hill gap. The car was not the root cause of his tardiness. Yes it was old, and yes it did break down a few times, but his tardiness was due to two self-admitted conditions. First, he did not like waking up before 10 a.m., and second, he liked the attention he got when he arrived at an event and everyone else was already there. This was a clear Will gap.

So why is diagnosing the right cause of this gap important? The answer to that question is the same for any performance gap. The wrong cause leads to the wrong solution and the wrong solution wastes money, time, and energy. Now I know my friend's parents loved him and would do almost anything to help him succeed in life, but not only did their solution fail to address the actual cause, it cost them more than was needed. They could have done several things to target the root cause of his tardiness. They could have called him each morning to get him out of bed. They could have paid me to make sure he got up. They could have given him $50 every morning he got to work on time. All of these solutions would likely have been more effective, would have cost less, and would probably have resulted in a longer lasting behavior change. Below is a little cost analysis of the various solutions.

Cause of Gap	Solutions to Gap	Cost of Gap
Hill	Buy a new car	$ 20,000 (one time)
Will	Parents wake-up call every morning	$ 36.50 ($0.10 a day for one year)
Will	Pay me to wake him up every day	$ 3,650 ($10 a day for one year)
Will	Reward him for everyday he was on time	$ 18,250 ($50 a day for one year)

The difference in cost between the various solutions ranged between $1,750 and $19,963.50 in potential savings. Now if the new car could succeed in decreasing my friend's tardiness the cost may not have mattered so much, but it could not because it was not the root cause of the gap. So, not only did they fail in changing his performance, but they wasted as much as $19,963.50 in the process.

So why did he and his parents get it so wrong? What was the Hill, Skill, or Will that kept them from seeing and addressing the real cause of his performance gap? If his parents were raging drunks or drug addicts, we could possibly blame their impaired mental processes (a Hill gap), but they weren't. If they were simply poor problem solvers and did not know what else to do (a Skill gap) we could point to that, but that did not seem to be the case either. What I recall most clearly points to something else as the likely cause. I seem to remember that his parents were extremely involved in managing, controlling, his life for him when he was living at home. Now that he was no longer under their roof, their ability to manage/control him was decreased and I suspect the new car was another way to reassert their influence (a Will gap). Unlike our next story, I do not know the truth behind why his parents did not see that the car was not the cause of his problem but regardless of whether my assumption is correct or not, they were not able to (Hill), did not know how to (Skill), or did not really want to (Will) address the true cause of the gap.

CUSTOMER SERVICE AGENTS

Some years ago, a business leader asked me to help her improve the performance of the organization's customer service agents. She had explained that the agents were making too many errors in documenting the information they collected from callers. In particular, they were missing several pieces of information in their call logs. Along with the description of the performance gap, she also told me she already assessed the situation and determined the solution she thought I should provide in order to improve the performance of these agents. She suggested I create a series of training simulations that could be used to re-train and test these employees on the proper way of documenting the information provided by callers. In other words, this leader (my client) had determined that these folks were not performing correctly because they didn't know or remember how and if they were just retrained it would solve the problem. In other words, they had a Skill gap.

On the surface it sounded like a reasonable and targeted solution for solving the performance gap they were experiencing. Unfortunately, it was nowhere close. Why? Because, it completely missed the true cause of the gap. After convincing this leader to give me a little time to do some analysis, I quickly discovered some very important aspects behind what was really happening. In talking with some of the customer service agents, I discovered that they all knew what was expected of them and were very capable of doing it correctly. In fact, they had all heard about the request the leader had made for retraining them and told me it would be a complete waste of time. So then, why all the errors?

Each month, the agents proceeded to tell me, an auditing team would provide a report to management that listed several metrics used in measuring their performance. If their performance met the established expectations, they kept their job, but if it fell below in certain areas over a period of time, they could be terminated. They also told me that over the past year, upper management had continuously (and unrealistically) revised the criteria and increased the expectations on how many calls were required to be handled. As these expectations grew they had started to see fellow agents let go for failing to meet the increases. So, in order to keep up with the new expectations, they had discovered and shared shortcuts in the processes that allowed them to complete more files than would otherwise be possible if they followed the procedures as they had previously learned.

Did these employees know how to correctly document the files? Yes, so they clearly did not have a Skill gap. Did they have all the computers, phones, forms, and materials needed to correctly document the files? Yes, so it was not a Hill gap. Did they care about meeting the expectations and documenting the files correctly of this particular business leader? No! Why? Because doing so could mean losing their jobs and most employees want to keep their jobs. Now you may be thinking, "But won't they start losing their jobs if they continue to make documentation errors?" Perhaps eventually, but up to this point the management that was making the firing decisions did not seem to care. No one had been fired for this reason and none of the agents saw any reason to be worried.

So what was the solution? Well, knowing that the primary cause of the performance gap was related to the lack of interest or desire by the agents to take fewer calls, the answer became pretty clear. Along with a few solutions that targeted other contributing factors, we needed to change the agents Wills. We needed to make it so that they wanted to complete the documentation correctly, and handle the expected number of calls. Unfortunately, that is not what happened, at least not until much later. What actually happened was:

- Recommendations (that did not include any training) were provided *and ignored*
- The original training solution was implemented *and failed*
- The recommendations were later revisited, implemented, *and successful*

To understand why this happened, the impact, and the importance it had to the company, we need to dive deeper into the story. To begin, let's examine the training solution in comparison to the recommendations that were provided. Then we will dive into the reasons why the correct solutions were ignored.

To implement the training solution, they had to contract with an outside company to creating the training materials. They had to take some time from an internal trainer to manage and implement the project. They had to assign and acquire the trainers and training resources (i.e. training rooms) needed to deliver the training and report testing results. Finally, and most importantly, the customer service agents had to stop answering the phones in order to attend the training. The general costs that were associated with this solution were as follows.

Material development	$100,000
Project management	$20,000
Trainer's time and resources	$5,000
Trainer's lost production time	$25,000
TOTAL	$150,000

In addition to above cost, there was no change in performance and the employees became resentful and frustrated for having been required to attend training unnecessarily.

In contrast, the recommendations that were provided did not include this, or any, training solutions. As explained, this was a Will gap and success would only come by changing the worthiness associated with performing as expected in the eyes of the agents found in. Now there are several ways this Will gap could have been resolved. The company could have:

- Rewarded agents that met the expected call quotas, but only when all their call documentation was completed accurately
- Revised the call quota expectations to allow for the time needed to complete the documentation correctly and meet the quota expectation
- Provided upper management with regular feedback, from the agents, regarding realistic workload expectations

What was officially recommended was a combination of the three, with a particular focus on the last two. I won't get into the specifics of the calculations but below are the cost comparisons.

Solutions to Gap	Cost of Solutions
Training solutions and tests	$150,000
Reward when done right (option 1)	$100,000
Revise quota expectations (option 2)	$5,000
Workload feedback to management (option 3)	$5,000

Even if all three non-training related options were implemented, the cost would have been $40,000 less than the training solution alone. More importantly, the only solutions that could resolve the performance gap were those that targeted the actual cause (the agent's wills). Eventually, this was realized by a broader management team and the company adopted the last two options, but why was this initially ignored? As explained in the previous chapter, other Hills, Skills, or Wills have a way of getting in the way of people being able to see or act on the true causes of a gap. In this case, there were two additional Wills and an additional Hill that got in the way.

Now I happen to believe there is value in the details of this story but in case you want to skip the details, I'll provide a summary explanation first. While the primary cause for the agents' performance gap was a lack of desire (a Will gap) to complete the call logs correctly, it became obscured by:

- Their manager's desire to prove to other managers (a second Will gap) that the agents already knew how to do the documentation correctly
- The company's upper management had mistakenly set an unrealistic performance expectation for the agents (a Hill gap)
- The manager knew the new expectation was unrealistic but was afraid to raise her concerns to upper management (a third Will gap).

The story is a bit like a soap opera but if you do not have the patience for all the detail you can skip to the final paragraph of this chapter. Otherwise, read on!

To more completely understand the background behind the misdiagnosis of this performance gap, let's look at the business context. In chapter 1, I explained how performance expectations can change significantly depending on the context (people and situation). In the business world there is generally more than one person involved in a performance situation, and more than one person's expectations that need to be considered. In this story, this directly contributed to and/or complicated the problem.

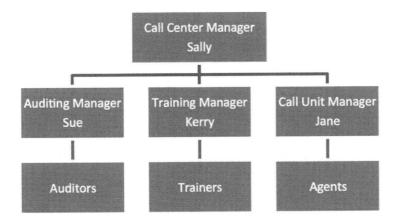

As you can see in the organizational chart above, there were several managers connected to the operation of the call center. The original request for help in improving the performance of the agents came from the Training Manager, Kerry. The Training Manger is responsible for making sure the agents are prepared to do their job correctly but the agents report to the Agent Manager, Jane, who is ultimately responsible for their job performance. An Auditing Manager, Sue, is responsible for the auditing team that tracks and reports the agent's performance metrics to all the managers in the group, particularly to the Call Center Manager, Sally, who is responsible for the overall call center operation and to whom all the other managers report.

It is also helpful to understand the relationships that existed between the managers. Below is a diagram that shows the relationships between the managers in the call center. The arrows show how they interact and the symbols represent the quality of the relationships between each of them. I have also provided a short description to give you a sense of the interactions and motivations for each the managers.

- \+ is a positive relationship
- \- is a negative relationship
- = is a relationship that is neither positive or negative

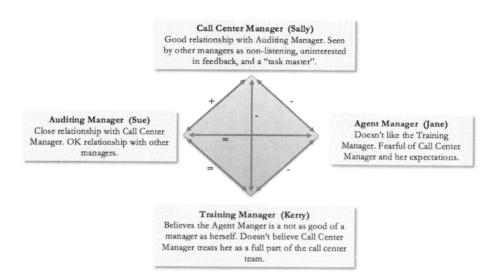

Now that you understand the organization and the relationships between the parties affecting the agents' job, you will understand how the correct performance solution in this example (and in many others) was overlooked and why.

As previously mentioned, the initial request for help to improve the agents' performance came to me from the Training Manager, Kerry. She did not indicate that any other managers were, or needed to be, involved and provided the proposed solution of creating training simulations before I had even started the process. Unknown to me at the time, and months before she engaged me, Sue, the Auditing Manger began informing all the managers in the group that the agents were missing an increasing amount of data from their call logs. In response to this news, the Call Center Manager, Sally, sent out a note to both the Agent Manager, Jane, and the Training Manager, Kerry, telling them how important it was for her center to maintain its successful track record and that they needed to investigate and resolve the issue. Jane did not believe that upper management's increased call expectations were realistic but rather than raising the issue with Sally, she blamed the issue on a lack of adequate training and began telling Kerry that they needed to provide more and better training immediately. As expected, Kerry reacted to this by defending the training that was previously given. She believed that the agents had been trained correctly and knew exactly how to do their jobs. She knew the agents were struggling with the increased call expectations and also believed the increased call expectations were unrealistic, but she also felt that part of the issue was due to the poor management skills of Jane. As previously explained, Kerry and Jane did not care much for each other to begin with, and both were afraid to engage Sally in the process. So, after months of blame and defense, Kerry decided that she would prove Jane wrong. She wanted to create and use the training simulation solution as a way to test the agents, prove to everyone that she had trained them correctly, get back at Jane for blaming her, and perhaps even build some credibility in the eyes of Sally.

Even though Kerry admitted that training simulations were not going to improve the agents' performance, she shielded the recommendation from the other managers and made the decision to move ahead with the training solution anyway. The others "needed to see" that she was right and that Jane was wrong. In the end, the simulations did much of what she had hoped they would. They showed that the agents knew what to do and that training was not the cause of the problems. Unfortunately, and as predicted, this did nothing to change the performance of the agents. The situation continued to fester for some months until the lack of change became more critical. At that point, Sally and upper management became aware of what Kerry had done and got more involved in the process.

This time the recommended solutions were considered by everyone (including the agents) and it was determined that the expectations had perhaps become a bit unrealistic. They saw merit in the option to reward the agents for the correct performance but since they had already wasted $150,000, they did not want to invest another $100,000. Instead, they relaxed the expectations on call numbers and increased expectations on collecting complete information from the callers. The gap was eventually bridged but money was wasted, time was lost, employees were frustrated, and both the Training and Agent Managers lost credibility in the eyes of the Call Center Manager.

Sadly, these stories are not isolated incidents. In fact, they are fairly average examples. Can you imagine business leaders spending millions of dollars on performance initiatives that completely miss or ignore the actual cause of a gap? It happens all the time in companies all over the world and it shows the importance in making sure you identify the real cause of performance gaps before taking action.

6. HOW TO RESOLVE THE GAPS

While all performance gaps are caused by Hills, Skills, and Wills, there are an unlimited number of solutions that can be used to resolve them. A single gap could have a thousand different ways in which people may choose to resolve it. However, there are a handful of approaches that have proven to increase success when developing those solutions. In preparation for the next chapter, we will discuss these approaches and which are best used when solving for a Hill, a Skill, or a Will.

MAKE SURE THE SOLUTION FITS

Let's start by quickly addressing one overarching principle to any solutions you develop and/or implement. The principle is simply this, don't try to force a square peg into a round hole. You need to make sure that every solution fits the environment and the people in it. Duh, you may say. Most people will admit that every situation and each performer is unique, but their actions often betray this. If every situation and person is unique, it means you cannot take a cookie cutter approach to the problem solving. Yet people everywhere continue to look back at the successes they had in past situations, and/or with past employers, and expect they will work again. Unfortunately, their assumptions are often wrong because they fail to make sure the solutions fit the new situation. Now, don't misunderstand what I am saying. There are occasions where a previous solution may work;

59

however, changes are almost always required in order for them to be successful again. It is when we refuse to consider "the fit" that problems arise. It always makes me cringe when I hear a business leader say, "I've done this before. All we need to do is…" I hear it all too often. I observed one of the worst instances of this a few years ago when an executive repeatedly used this exact quote. While he was responsible for implementing a strategic initiative that would affect the entire future of the business, he refused to listen to the advice of other executives and professional specialists. He ignored their recommendations and their concerns about the "fit" of his solutions in this organization. When he was challenged, he used intimidation to push ahead with his ideas. When problems arose he blamed others for the failures, even though they had told him his ideas were not going to work. As I write this down, the project is over a year behind schedule, with several more required before it will be completed. Several people have been blamed for the delays and "let go." Several more left the company to escape the situation, the company had to cut their expenses by $40 million dollars to make up for the delays, and the company is now in real danger of being taken over by a competitor or going out of business. Now to be fair, other factors (i.e. the struggling economy) have had some impact on the situation but a significant portion of this organization's problems rest with this one executive's steadfast mindset of "I've done this before. All we need to do is _____."

Having discussed the importance of making sure solutions "fit the situation," the remainder of this chapter will look at five different approaches that are helpful when developing solutions that target Hills, Skills, and Wills. They are:

1. Leverage every resource
2. Make sure it's understood and meaningful
3. Remove negative consequences for good behavior
4. Remove positive rewards for bad behavior
5. Make it easier

LEVERAGE EVERY RESOURCE

This approach to developing solutions is particularly well suited when addressing both Hill and Skill gaps, and while it is not particularly profound, there are two aspects I want to highlight that can expand the way you look at resources and increase the number and quality of the solutions you develop.

The first of these is to think broadly about resources. Notice that the approach is to leverage every resource. Most people think of resources as tangible or physical items such as money, objects, and people. But if they stop there, they limit the resources they can use to develop potential solutions. Resources can also be non-physical and by broadening the way you think of resources you can broaden your potential solutions. A great example of this is time. Time is not a physical resource (though some scientists may challenge me on that), but having more or less of it can make a significant difference in performance. If I work longer, I can_____. Another example of a non-physical resource is quality. I can't hold quality but I can increase or decrease it, and doing so can make a significant difference in performance. Can you see how thinking broadly about resources can help? Let's say you make suit coats but because of some new competition you now need to make them at 10% less than what you were spending before. Some solutions that consider physical resources to overcome the Hill gap could be:

- Money: pay your workers less
- People: layoff some workers
- Objects: use more efficient (faster and less energy) sewing machines

But you could also consider solutions that leverage non-physical resources:

- Time: work extra hours
- Quality/Process: single stitching instead of double.

Other resources (physical and non-physical) could include; geography, expertise, reputation, brand recognition, and intellectual property, but regardless of what resources you may come up with, thinking more broadly about resources can expand the list of solutions that could potentially bridge your performance gaps.

Now let's look at the second of the two aspects I mentioned. Again, notice that the approach is to leverage every resource. It does not say to leverage every available resource. We not only need to broaden what we consider to be a resource, but we need to broaden our thinking about what resources we may acquire. Just because you don't have the resource does not mean you cannot leverage it.

No person is an island. You do not have to solve the gap on your own or without the aid of others resources. In fact, to do so may just be plain foolishness. Sometimes the resources you may need can come from the most unlikely places. Have you ever heard the expression, "your enemy's enemy is your friend?" History is punctuated with instances where countries that dislike each other will join forces, or give their resources to the other, because they share a common enemy (i.e. WWII era U.S.A. and U.S.S.R.). Family, friends, acquaintances, strangers, even enemies may be willing provide you resources to help get you past your Hill and Skill gaps.

A few years ago I read an interesting story on the internet[1] that highlights both these aspects of leveraging every resource. It started in 2005 as a hobby. An unemployed, 26-year-old Canadian, Kyle MacDonald, wanted to acquire a house. The gap was that he didn't have one. What resources did/didn't he have? Well he had no job and no money to purchase a home. He did have a red paper clip, a website, and plenty of time. He also had an entire planet of other people that both have and want "stuff." Over the course of one year this young man took his paper clip and traded his way up until he eventually had a home of his own. At first he traded his paper clip to two women from Vancouver, Canada, for a fish pen. From there he traded up to a door knob, then a camping stove, a generator, an instant party, a snowmobile, a trip to Yahk, British Columbia, a van, a recording contract, a year of rent in Phoenix, AZ, an afternoon with rocker Alice Cooper, and then a rare snow globe. At that point he was contacted by actor Corbin Bernsen, who apparently collects snow globes, and in exchange offered him a paid role in his new movie. Finally, the city of Kipling, Saskatchewan, Canada, wanted the movie role and offered him a farm house.

This is an amazing example of how someone can use a resource that most would dismiss and leverage the resources of others to overcome a significant Hill gap. It would also be just as effective in resolving a Skill gap if he had wanted to learn guitar or acquire some acting skills. The point is that leveraging every resource (physical, non- physical, yours, and others) is a key approach when looking for solutions to performance gaps caused by Hills or Skills.

Make Sure It's Understood And Meaningful

The next approach for developing solutions is particularly suited for targeting Skill and Will gaps. It is to ensure that the expected performance is understood and meaningful to those expected to do it. Let's start by explaining why the expected performance needs to be understood and what that means.

How can someone meet an expectation if they don't know what it is? In case you need me to say it, the answer is they can't! Sometimes the only thing keeping people from doing what is expected, is not knowing what is expected. This should always be the first piece of information you check for when considering if performers are experiencing a Skill gap. It is also the

---

1   Muir, David. "Man Trades Up From Paper Clip to House." ABC News 09 July 2006

easiest to be fixed. By identifying solutions that clarify the expectations, and any need to remind performers of the expectations, you can quickly and easily improve performance.

Another aspect of understanding the expected performance is knowing whether it is being met or not. Performers may know what is expected, but if they cannot see how they are doing they may go too far or not far enough. For example, have you ever heard the story of Florence May Chadwick? In 1952, Florence tried to swim from Catalina Island to the California coastline, a 26 miles distance. After swimming for 16 hours, and in a thick fog, she gave up. Shortly after she got out of the ocean, she discovered that she was only one mile from the California shore. If only she had been able to see through the fog the outcome may have been quite different. Two months later she tried again and succeeded.

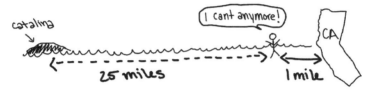

Being able to see how we are progressing toward a goal or expectation can impact our performance as dramatically as it did for Florence. As such, we not only need to make sure we clarify the expectations to the performers, but we need to make sure they can see their progress, and if they can't, we need to develop solutions that will allow them to.

The final part of this approach is to make sure the performers see the expectation as meaningful in some form. Now this does not mean the performers need to be willing to sacrifice their lives in order to achieve the expectation, although in some cases it could (i.e. military service). Humans do, however, need to be able to find some benefit or logical reasoning behind their work or actions, even if the reasoning is flawed. We (particularly adults) strive for meaning in all we do, and when it does not exist or is unclear, our motivation to perform suffers. Now, I hope not to offend anyone by using such an extreme example to illustrate this point, but I want to share it because it paints a very clear and vivid picture of how important meaning is to us as humans. I read this story over 20 years ago and the point it made is just as clear today as it was then. The story was written by a former convict and Christian prison reformer, Dr. Charles Colson. In it, he tells about an experiment that was conducted in a Hungarian concentration camp during WWII. In the account, a Nazi officer commanded his prisoners to shovel dirt into carts, move it to the other end of the camp, and put it in a pile.

Although they were undernourished and weak, the prisoners worked hard and completed their task by that evening. The following day, the officer ordered them to move the same pile back across the camp to where they had taken it from. Again, they did so. Each day they were ordered to move the pile of dirt back. After several weeks, prisoners began going mad, crying and screaming. Some were beaten until they stopped crying. Some ran into the camp fence and were electrocuted, and others ignored the guard's calls to stop and were shot. I can't honestly imagine how anyone could conduct such a cruel experiment but I am not surprised by the results. People need meaning! It doesn't have to be a lot but the more their meaning is taken away, the more their performance will suffer.

Often, the reason people do not care about doing what is expected (a Will gap) is because they simply do not see any, or enough, meaning in what they are told or being asked to do. Again, the key is to make sure the performers see and understand the expectation as meaningful. The more meaningful it is to them (not you) the better your chances of improving performance. To convince you of the truth of this, let's try a little test. On the next page are two scenarios, business and personal, where performance improvement is needed. Read each scenario and the three performance expectations directly below it, then rank the expectations in the order that would motivated the best performance from you.

BUSINESS SCENARIO:	PERSONAL SCENARIO:
You are a seamstress for a uniform clothing company. You sew 45 uniforms every day. You're paid minimum wage and typically work 8 hours a day to complete the work.	You are 40-years-old. You're overweight. You're married and have 3 kids in school. You spend 60 hours of each week at a stressful job.
1. Management just explained that you are now expected to sew 5 extra uniforms each day for the next month.	1. You just had your annual physical and the doctor says you need to lose some weight.
2. Management just explained that you are now expected to sew 5 extra uniforms each day (for the next month) and will be paid overtime to complete the extra 5 uniforms.	2. You just had your annual physical and the doctor says you are likely to have a heart attack in the next year if you do not lose 50 pounds.
3. Management just explained that they want volunteers to sew 5 extra uniforms each day (for the next month) because one of their clients (a hospital) just opened 1,000 clinics to provide free medical services for children with terminal cancer. All the buildings, materials, and doctor services are being donated and the company wants to donate the uniforms but cannot afford to hire more people or pay extra for the work.	3. You just had your annual physical and the doctor says you are likely to have a heart attack in the next year if you do not lose 50 pounds. Your children hear you discussing this with your spouse. When tucking in your youngest child that night, they start crying and tell you that they do not want you to die and that they are scared.

Did you select the first option in either scenario? Of all the people I have asked/interviewed, not one has selected either of the first options as their first choice. The reason is because the second and third options provide a context for meaning that people can easily find value in. The first option in both scenarios does not give any context for meaning and leaves the performer in the position to either assume there is none or to come up with their own. Both of these outcomes are dangerous. By failing to explain the context of a new expectation, many people will have a tendency to assume negative intent. They may assume that the reason they are expected to work longer is because the CEO just wants to get richer or doesn't care about the wellbeing of his/her employees. In cases where no meaning is assumed, important information that can affect performance gets missed. For instance, in the personal scenario, if you simply assumed the doctor was telling you to lose weight because that's just what doctors are supposed to say to overweight people, you could be missing important information that could potentially save your life.

So how can we help make sure performers understand the meaning behind the expected performance? Asking one or two questions can help achieve this. Each has a different perspective but both get to the core of meaning. The first is, "What's in it for me?" I believe that humans are, by nature, self-serving. That we only do things that we find some personal benefit or meaning in doing. As such, performers need to know what they will get out of meeting the expectation. Will I make more money? Will I gain more prestige? Will I keep my job? Will I stay alive? On the flip side, humans also have the capacity to gain benefit or meaning from sacrificially giving to others. This is where the second question comes in. "What's in it for us?" We can and do sometimes place our focus on others, but even in those instances the performer must still find personal meaning behind it. "Us" includes "Me." For example, I may choose to help sick people over making more money or choose to die for my country, but the reason I am willing to do these things for others is because I still find some value in them for myself. The minute I find out that the sick person is faking their illness or the country I am serving is committing some atrocity against its own people, the meaning will be lost and my performance will change.

As you develop solutions to address people's understanding of the expected performance and its meaning or value, you need to remember to make sure they "fit." Different people find meaning in different things. While previous performers may have valued money more than service, others may not. But, by making sure performers, and those setting the performance expectation, understand "What's in it for me," and "What's in it for us," you ensure that they find some meaning in meeting the expectation.

REMOVE NEGATIVE CONSEQUENCES FOR EXPECTED PERFORMANCE

The three remaining approaches to creating effective solutions specifically target Will gaps. The first of these is to remove negative consequences for good performance.

Sometimes doing the worthwhile/desired/expected thing can result in negative outcomes that are punishing to performers, and will cause them to stop or decrease their performance. A common occurrence of this in organizations is the employee who does difficult and/or additional work so well that their manager continues to give them more, even though the employee doesn't want or like the work. Managers will typically refer to the work as "career opportunities," even if they are not. In one case, an executive continued to give one of their employees additional work assignments outside their normal job responsibilities. The employee was very good at the tasks and happy to help at first, but as the assignments kept flowing in he grew more and more frustrated. Eventually it got to the point where he hated going to work, so he left. Unfortunately, the organization not only lost a high performing employee but that employee left to go work for a competitor and took a few other employees with him. The problem here was not that the employee was unable to meet the performance expectation. The problem was that he felt punished for meeting it.

Negative consequences for meeting performance expectations can occur anywhere. Spending less money than your department originally budgeted may result in being given a smaller budget next year. Employees that offer suggestions in meetings may get assigned the responsibility to carry them out. Getting better grades in high school may decrease a student's social status with friends. Staying alive may mean you can't eat shellfish anymore.

Now in some cases the negative consequences are so small that there is no impact on the expected performance, but as the negative consequences grow bigger so do their impact on the expected performance. I don't think there is anyone who loves the taste of lobster so much that they are willing to die for it. However, I have witnessed people who will choose death over the continued side effects of certain cancer treatments. When there are negative consequences for doing what is expected, performance will be impacted at some level.

To resolve these types of Will gaps, you could add a positive benefit that is meaningful enough to overshadow the negative consequences. In instances where employees are tempted to leave because managers are pushing additional or difficult work on them, some employers have offered pay increases, promises of promotion, service awards, and a host of other incentives. Sometimes these do work for a while but the problem with this approach however is that the additional incentives tend to be short lived. The negative consequence is still there and frequently reemerges; ending in a return to the performance gap you started with. The best way to resolve these types of Will gaps is to identify and, if possible, remove the negative consequences altogether. In the example of the employee who left the organization because the manager continued to give him more "career opportunities," removing or just reducing the additional work would have allowed the employee to continue doing what they wanted, and were hired, to do. The executive could probably have still benefited by using the employee on some assignments and the employee would have stayed at the organization, as would those he took with him. As such, removing the negative consequence is the best approach if possible, followed closely by reducing the negative consequences.

REMOVE POSITIVE REWARDS FOR UNWANTED PERFORMANCE

The fourth approach is almost the mirror opposite of the previous. Instead of removing negative consequences for good performance, you remove positive rewards for unwanted performance. Sometimes organizations and individuals find themselves in situations where they have actually put some process or incentive in place that encourages their performers to behave in a way that is contrary to what they ultimately want. For instance, if a company paid you $500 for selling one computer and $200 for selling two, how many would you try to sell? Most people would only sell one, and while you may think this situation would never happen, it is actually just an overly simplified example based on hundreds of true stories where performers have actually been encouraged to perform in a way contrary to what is expected or desired.

Just recently I read of another example where this took place. Suffering from people's declining trust in financial institutions, a company made it one of their primary goals to improve their customer satisfaction numbers. At the same time, the sales leadership of this company decided to launch a new program that financially rewarded managers based on the number of products they sold to their clients. To be clear, there was nothing wrong with this program in itself but it ended up encouraging the wrong behaviors in their managers. Managers began selling whatever product they could, in order to increase compensation, even if it was not a good fit for the buyer. In the end, the company's customer satisfaction went down and they succeeded in lowering trust instead of improving it.

It's not too difficult to find examples of this behavior in organizations, and the same is true in people's personal lives. Have you ever seen a child who has learned that throwing a tantrum will cause their parents to give them what they want? Regardless of where these situations take place, the best approach to resolving them is to simply remove the incentive (the positive reward) that is encouraging people to do what you don't want or expect. In the case of the first example, you could make the incentive for selling one computer $100 instead of $500. Likewise, in the second example, you could specify that all products sold must be a good fit, as measured by their customer's satisfaction ratings. Both these actions remove the rewards associated with the undesired behavior and would improve performance.

On a side note, one of the challenges I have noticed with understanding the approach of removing rewards for unwanted performance is that people can sometimes mistake it with the development of punishments. For example, some managers view the continued employment of people that are not meeting their expectations as a form of rewarding them for the wrong behaviors. As such, they can also see the firing of these employees as the removal of that positive reward. In some cases they may be right. Firing an employee for not doing their job may ultimately be a solution, but sometimes people resort to intimidation and coercion to try and drive performance. Intimidation and coercion are all too common tactics by people trying to get others to do what they want, but, while it may stop the person from doing X, it won't necessarily encourage them to do Y. Creating deterrents can be a valid approach to modifying behavior but it is not all that effective when trying to improve performance. When people are sincerely trying to meet performance expectations, identifying and removing positive rewards is more effective than the threat of punishment.

MAKE IT EASIER

The fifth and final approach in my list could alternatively be viewed as an approach to solve Hill, Skill, or Will gaps. The deciding factor of where it fits is dependent on your perspective, but I view it as ultimately resolving a Will gap because the core issue seems to revolve around an unwillingness to do things under certain circumstances. Let me explain this further.

When tasks are, or are perceived as being, too difficult, humans can have a tendency to purposely avoid them. This can be a debilitating problem when the expected performance is a single task (i.e. flossing your teeth) but performance expectations often involve a series of tasks (i.e. taking care of your teeth) and the avoidance of just one of them can also negatively impact the outcome of the rest.

Notice how I said perceived as being too difficult? Tasks may not actually be too difficult, or even slightly difficult, but if performers perceived them this way, avoidance behaviors may begin to take shape in a variety of ways. They can take the form of overt avoidance, such as refusing to do the task. It could result in putting the task off until the last possible minute. Or, it could manifest in the task being done in a less than perfect manner. The greater the difficulty or perception of difficulty, the stronger the avoidance tendency can become.

Now, you could try to convince the performers that the tasks are not really that difficult but that is like trying to convince your 4-year-old child that Brussels sprouts actually taste just as good as chocolate. The better approach is to actually try and make the tasks easier, if possible. For example, I personally struggled with taking care of my teeth for much of my life.

I brushed pretty consistently but routinely skipped dentist appointments and only flossed on the day or two before I actually visited the Dentist. As expected, over the years I had developed some fairly serious gum diseases (i.e. Periodontitis, Gingivitis) that were the direct result of my avoidance of flossing. One day, I finally decided to take the time to apply my own performance methods to this issue. I already knew the importance of flossing, the potential dangers of not flossing, and how to floss properly, so I was able to rule out any Skill gaps. I also owned several containers of floss and everything else needed to floss, so I ruled out any Hill gaps. This left me with a Will gap. As I started exploring my Will to floss, I discovered that though I had some genuine desire to change, I simply found the task to be too much of an inconvenience. I didn't like having to get out the floss container from under the bathroom sink. I didn't like rolling floss around my fingers and I didn't like getting them covered in saliva. So as part of the overall solution I tried to remove the things I did not like by making flossing easier. I bought some floss sticks so I didn't have to stick my fingers in my mouth. I also put the picks in an easily accessible container on the counter next to my toothbrush so I didn't have to do anything extra to get the floss. As a result, several years have passed and I am still flossing almost every day. My gum problems have all but disappeared and my dentist (whom I still doesn't particularly like to visit but don't avoid anymore) has even commented on how he wished his other patients had such healthy teeth and gums.

This example may seem silly, but I hope you can see how difficult tasks (real or perceived) can lead people to not want to perform as expected. Making tasks easier can help solve this Will gap, but this approach can work equally well in solving Hill or Skill gaps. As mentioned, the differentiator is your perspective. To keep this brief, you could:

- Look at it as a sub-approach to a Will gap by saying that making something easier is just another way to remove the negative consequences they experience when doing what is expected
- Say that since making something easier often requires providing additional resources, or the removal of obstacles, is it just another way to overcome an obstacle (a Hill gap)
- Say that one way to making something easier is to provide better information or training so people have the skills and knowledge required (a Skill gap)

Regardless of how you look at it, making things easier can help performers overcome their gaps and improve their performance.

7. PROCESS AND PRACTICE

At this point, you should be ready to take what you now know and put it into practice. You have a basic understanding of human behavior, you have answered the question of whether or not you believe change is possible, you have seen how every performance gap (including the reason they are misdiagnosed or ignored) is caused by one or more Hill, Skill, and Will, and you have learned several approaches that can help to develop solutions that target these gaps. The last two things you need to succeed in applying all this information, whether in practice or real life, is a process to follow and an opportunity practice. In this chapter you will receive both.

Having a curious personality and a bit of knowledge is important but, make no mistake, analyzing performance gaps is a process. In this chapter, I will introduce you to the HSW Performance Analysis Worksheet. This worksheet will guide you through an analysis process that is built around the Hills, Skills, and Wills methodology. I will demonstrate how the worksheet is used in real performance situations and give you the opportunity to practice using it on your own performance improvement needs.

As you become familiar with the HSW worksheet, you may come to think it would work even better by making a few tweaks. If so, go ahead! Experimentation is one of the most effective ways we humans learn, but first try to follow it a few times as it is. The worksheet was designed to both follow the process and to teach it. As such, each step, question, instruction, and action is there for a reason. But, regardless of whether you use it, tweak it, or something else, find one that works for you and to stick with it. Following a well thought out process will not only allow you to spend more time focusing on the end result (rather than the process), it will help you avoid making mistakes.

Now, before we jump into the HSW Performance Analysis Worksheet there are a few brief pointers I want to highlight regardless of the process you use. A good process will already have these embedded within it but even when they are included, people can overlook their importance. For this reason, I believe they are worth mentioning. First, you need to be as specific as possible in your answers. Statements like, "they need to improve" or "they need to understand" are useless when trying to identify the cause of problems or when developing solutions. Instead, be specific. Close your eyes and visualize what you would see the performers doing if they "understood" or "improved." Would seeing someone turn down a bribe prove to you that they "understood" your company's value of integrity? Would you consider a group's performance to have "improved" if you saw them stacking boxes more quickly? These are the specifics you want and need to capture. The more specific you can be, the more likely your chances are of identifying the right gaps and solutions. The second point when using any performance analysis process is to make sure you include others in the process. If the process you are following does not include this you are walking on some very thin ice. I don't care how many years of experience you have had or how smart you think you are, analyzing performance gaps is a team sport. As previously discussed, not involving others can often lead to misdiagnosing the cause of the gaps and wasting your money, time, and energy pursuing solutions that fix the wrong things. The third and final point I want to highlight is related to the second. As you start involving others in your analysis, you frequently find that the information you collect will change over time. This is normal! In fact, changes in your analysis often indicate the places where you have just avoided making a costly mistake. You should update your analysis comments as much as needed. You should also make sure you do not dismiss or lose the older information. Keeping all your information provides additional insights regarding the gap by allowing you to see how the analysis changes over time. You can manage old and new data in different ways. You can assign dates to each comment. You can even strikeout old comments and then add new ones. Some may prefer using a separate worksheet for each person they involve in the process. Others may prefer to use one worksheet, placing everyone's comments within it. Experiment and find the way that works best for you personally, but make sure you don't lose sight of older information as you discover and capture new ones.

OK, now that the pointers have been addressed, we can jump into learning and practicing how to use the HSW Performance Analysis Process. In the back of this book is a blank copy of the HSW Performance Analysis Worksheet. You can also download free copies from the Hills, Skills, and Wills Facebook page or from the website for my business coaching practice, www.cornerstonebec.com. It is specifically designed around the Hills, Skills, and Wills methodology and will guide you through the process of analyzing performance problems. The worksheet is broken down into three major sections, each of which contains a series of questions that will focus on the areas listed above. As we walk through each section, I will explain its purpose and importance, demonstrate how it is used, and give you the opportunity to practice using it on a performance gap of your choosing. Lets get started!

SECTION 1: Getting Started
1. Clearly understand what the performance gap is
2. Know who it affects and should be involved in the analysis
3. Are confident the expected performance is possible
4. Determine whether it's worth doing anything about
SECTION 2: Causes and Solutions
5. Identify all the causes of the gap
6. Avoid misdiagnosis or ignoring potential causes
7. Identify targeted solution(s) for each cause
SECTION 3: Defining your Plan
8. Select the best possible solution(s) to implement

SECTION 1: GETTING STARTED

If you fail to aim, you're aiming to fail. The "Getting Started" section of the worksheet is designed to make sure you aim before jumping headlong into something you, and others, may not really understand or agree upon. It will help you to collect some foundational information and focus your thinking and actions throughout the rest of the worksheet and performance analysis process. This section includes four steps:

1. Clearly defining the performance gap
2. Identifying who is affected and should be involved in the analysis process

3. Determining whether the expected performance is possible
4. Deciding if it is really worth doing anything about.

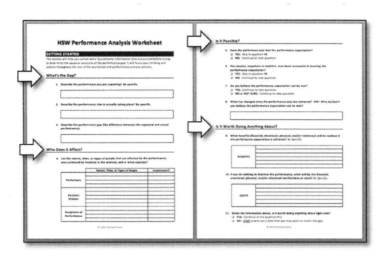

STEP 1: What's The Gap?

In the first focus area, you define the expected performance, the performance that is actually taking place, and the gap (the difference between the two). Now your performance issue may seem so obvious that documenting it feels like a waste of time, but you would be wrong. Sometimes we think things are obvious until we are forced to describe them. We then realize they aren't quite as obvious as we thought. The process of writing it down helps us to clarify our expectations and sometimes identify additional expectations that we did not initially consider. More importantly, documenting this information is important because in the midst of the process there is often a tendency to stray off course. Having the expectation, the actual performance, and the performance gap in writing gives you a clear view where the center of your target lies and can alert you if things start straying off course. Having this target clearly defined can also help you assess whether your solutions are aiming at the intended target. For instance, consider the following example.

I worked with two large companies that both wanted to implement a performance management process. The expectation was to improve both employee and company performance by making sure everyone knew exactly what work activities they needed to do, how well they accomplished those activities, and how each activity aligned with the overall goals the company was trying to achieve. This would make sure everyone was "rowing in the same direction" and ultimately improve the company's performance. Unfortunately, when we started developing solutions, leaders began proposing and insisting on solutions that targeted other expectations and desires, many of which actually had negative effects on the expected performance. Most of the leaders wanted reports that listed everyone's work activities, and which company goals they aligned to. One leader wanted to see reports that ranked how well people performed their goals in comparison to others. Another wanted to assign performance rating numbers to everyone because it would make the reporting more efficient. Another wanted to use the rating numbers to determine how much of a raise employees would receive. And, another wanted to force every manager to assign 10% of their team with the highest rating and 10% with a lowest rating. Now there is nothing wrong, with these additional expectations. Identifying additional expectations can help improve the final results, but they can also hinder and even destroy performance. One of the Chief Human Resource Officers I worked with had a clever term for this phenomena that has stuck with me for years. He called this the "Christmas tree" effect. The idea was, you start with a beautiful Christmas tree, then people start adding more and more ornaments on the tree until it eventually starts to bend over and sag from the extra weight. The Christmas tree no longer looks (or functions) like a Christmas tree should. The leaders in both these companies where not on the same page, and rather than developing a solution that targeted their primary expectation, they threw everything on the tree and created a solution that many of them did not even follow.

Demonstration

On the next page is an example showing how to complete this step in the worksheet using the Customer Service Agent scenario we discussed in Chapter 5. This example also demonstrates the first of the three pointers we discussed at the start of this chapter. While they were somewhat vague, the initial answers were not erased.

HILLS, SKILLS, AND WILLS

What's the Gap?

1. Describe the performance you are expecting? Be specific.

> ~~Customer Services Agents need to complete their call logs~~.
> Customer Services Agents need to handle 40 calls each day AND
> ensure all the required fields are completed in each call log.

2. Describe the performance that is actually taking place? Be specific.

> ~~Customer Services Agents are not completing their call logs.~~ Cus-
> tomer Services Agents are handling 40 calls each day but several
> required fields in the call logs are being left incomplete or blank.

3. Describe the performance gap (the difference between the expected and actual performance).

> ~~Customer Services Agents need to complete their call logs.~~ Cus-
> tomer Services Agents need to complete all required fields in their
> call logs.

Once more people were interviewed and it became clear that the expectation included both completion of the required fields in the logs and maintaining a certain call quota. The previous notes were crossed out and updated with more specific information. The example also shows how the gap is the DIFFERENCE between the expected and actual performance. The expected performance was that they needed to handle 40 calls AND complete the call log fields. Since the agents were already handling 40 calls a day, the only gap was that they needed to complete the required call log fields.

***

Your Turn!

Take a few minutes to stop and think about a personal or organizational performance challenge you are currently facing. Use a blank copy of the worksheet and complete the "What's the Gap" step.

***

STEP 2: WHO DOES IT AFFECT?

In the second step of the "Getting Started" section, you identify the people that are affected by the performance and indicate how they will be, or were, involved in the process. The importance of this step is related to the second of the three pointers we discussed. It will help you avoid or decrease the possibility of misdiagnosing the cause of the gap by identifying other people that should be involved in the analysis process.

Demonstration

Using the Customer Service Agent example again, you can see how the identification of additional people to involve grew over time.

Who Does it Affect?

4. List the names, titles, or types of people that are affected by the performance, which have been involved in the analysis, and in what capacity?

	Names, Titles, or Typs of People	Interviewed?
Performers	100 Customer Service Agents	Interviewed (10)
Decision Makers	Training Manager	Interviewed and Reviewed Analysis
	Agent Manager	Interviewed and Reviewed Analysis
	Audit Manager	Interviewed and Reviewed Analysis
	Call Center Manager	Interviewed and Reviewed Analysis
	VP Operations	Reviewed Analysis
Recipients of Performance	Customers	

When the analysis first began the only people considered were the Training Manager (who requested the help), the Agents (who had the gap), and the customers. But, as the Agents were interviewed it became clearer that others were impacted by the performance and should be involved in making decisions regarding it, so the table was updated to include; the Agent Manager, Audit Manager, Call Center Manager, and the VP of Call Center Operations. I sometimes indicate the original people involved with yellow highlighting but you can select any method that works best for you.

This table also seeks to indicate the involvement type for each individual or group. Are they decision makers or just people to gather information from? Some performance consultants may prefer to be more detailed here and include several involvement types but I find it helpful to keep the involvement types to the two most critical; those you have, or will, interview and those you have, or will, review the analysis with. Again, you should experiment with the worksheet to find a method that works best for you.

As a side note, notice that even though Customers were included as a people group affected by the performance gap, they were not involved in the analysis. It is always best to include every group affected by the performance. Even if you do not include them in your analysis at this time, you might revisit the analysis and include them later. Customers are often a critical part of analyzing business performance gaps but, as in this case, they are often left out of the equation for a host of reasons, such as not having enough time, not wanting to inconvenience them, or simply overlooking them.

> **Your Turn!**
> Stop and consider who is affected by the performance gap you identified in the previous practice exercise. Take the worksheet you started and complete the "Who Does it Affect" step.

STEP 3: IS IT POSSIBLE?

The next step in the "Getting Started" section seeks to identify whether the expected performance is actually possible, as well as the rationale for that answer. This step consists of four questions but you may not need to answer them all, so be sure to follow the directions carefully. The flowchart below shows how your answers during this step will determine which questions you complete.

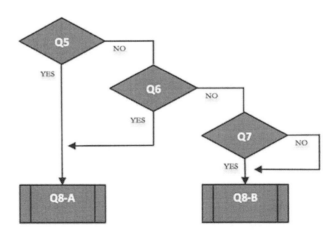

You should also note that each question refers to your "performance expectations" and not just the "performance gap." This is important because expectations and gaps are not always the same. As our Customer Service Agent example demonstrated, the expectation was to answer 40 calls each day AND complete all the required fields. The gap was only completion of the required fields.

The first question in this step seeks to determine whether the performers have ever previously met the expectation. Have they ever changed a flat tire? Have they ever sold 100 computers? Have they ever _____? If your answer is YES, congratulations! Given a positive response, there is no need to answer the next two questions in this step. The expectation is most definitely possible because the performers have done it before. There is one final question to consider before you finish this step however, as it will begin to focus your attention on some key aspects of the situation. We will get to this question soon but before we do, lets consider the opposite response. Say your answer to the question is NO. The performers have never met the expectation before. Answering NO does not mean the performance expectation is impossible. After all, just because someone hasn't changed a flat tire, or sold 100 computers doesn't mean they can't. This response will therefore lead you to the second question.

The second question in this step expands the scope of the first by looking at whether others have ever met the expectation. If others, at any point in history, have been able to meet the expectation, then it is possible. This response brings you to the same point as if you answered YES to the first question. It also results in your being directed to skip ahead and answer a final question before completing the step. However, let's again consider the opposite response. Say that no one has ever met the expectation. Even if this is the case, it is still not quite fair to say that the expectation is impossible to be met. After all, people used to say we couldn't put a man on the moon and I think we all know how that turned out. This takes us to the third question.

If no one has ever before met the expected performance, you need to do a reality check. This is the sole purpose of the third question. Do you really believe it is possible? Whether you respond YES or NO there is telling information behind each response and you will be instructed to consider that in the last question.

The fourth and final question is sort of a cheat. It is really two questions but you only need to answer the one you are instructed to by your responses in the worksheet. The reason for this is twofold. If you answered YES to the first or second questions you not only know that that the expectation is possible, but you should realize that something must have changed between the time when the performers could meet the expectation and now that they aren't. Something is different, and identifying those differences can point you in the direction of some potential causes and/or solutions to the gap. Likewise, if you made it to the third question, there are always reasons why people believe something is or is not possible. These reasons can also point you in the direction of some potential causes and/or solutions to the gap.

I am always surprised when individuals or business leaders set expectations having given little to no though about whether those expectations were realistic. There are lots of reasons for this but how valuable would it be to know why a group of performers don't believe your expectation is possible to be met? Likewise, how valuable would be to know the differences between a group that is meeting an expectation and one that isn't? How much money, time, and headaches could having this information save you?

DEMONSTRATION

Below are the answers to these questions in the customer service example we began. Starting with the first question, and after multiple interviews, it became clear that the Agents had never met this specific expectation before.

Is it Possible?

5. Have the performers ever met the performance expectation?

   ☐ **YES**: Skip ahead and answer question #8A
   ☒ **NO**: Continue to next question #6

6. Has anyone, anywhere or anytime, ever been successful in meeting the performance expectation?

   ☐ **YES**: Skip ahead and answer question #8A
   ☒ **NO**: Continue to next question #7

7. Do you believe the performance expectation can be met?

   ☐ **YES**: Answer question #8B
   ☒ **NO** or **NOT SURE**: Answer question #8B

8. A) What has changed since the performance was last achieved? B) Why do/don't you believe the performance expectation can be met?

   > Not sure it can be met. Never met before. Most Agents do not believe the expectation is realistic. Agents have met all previous expectations but have repeatedly complained about **increasing call quotas**. **Not enough time** for calls and all other tasks.

This directs us to the second question. Had others ever met the expectation? Many of the Agents had been with the company for several years and, to the best of their knowledge, no one anywhere else ever had. Following the instructions to this response, the third question was asked and what was uncovered was that the majority of Agents were not at all confident the expectation was possible. Some were even sure it was not and had vocalized their concerns previously. This led to part B of the final question. In asking why they did not believe the expectation was possible, it became clearer that time and the increasing call quotas were their key reasons.

Your Turn!

Interview yourself regarding the performance expectation you identified and complete the "Is It Possible?" step.

Remember to include others as well when able.

STEP 4: Is It Worth Doing Anything About?

If you have to spend $10 to make $1, is it worth it? The answer is….maybe! Many times people invest in efforts that have little value in the end. We do this for a host of reasons; but regardless, checking that the performance is really worth doing anything about is one of the smartest things you can do. This is the purpose of the last focus area in the "Getting Started" section. Now, since we have not yet fully engaged in identifying the causes and solutions of the gap, this will just be an initial assessment. We will revisit this again toward the end of the worksheet, as the cost for some of the solutions we develop may change our decisions. Regardless, starting to look at this question now may provide enough information for you to determine whether it is worth going any further.

Worth is ultimately determined by considering the costs and benefits of an action. Sometimes costs and benefits are simply the mirror image of each other, but other times they are completely independent of each other. Looking at both of these is important to capture a complete picture, so we begin by having you consider the expectation and list all the positive benefits you and others expect to get by achieving it. The first question directs you to think of benefits from four perspectives: Financial, Emotional, Relational, and Physical. Financial benefits are pretty straight forward. For instance, you may save a million dollars. Since we are emotional beings, emotions are often an equally important benefit, and frequently overlooked. For instance, you may become more liked or feel more satisfied. Relational benefits are closely related but I mention them separately to highlight that fact that emotional benefits can stem internally and externally. We all want to be loved, to be happy, or to feel secure but, our relationships with others can lead us closer or further from those feelings. The last perspective to consider is physical benefits. These include our health and safety. This is one of humanities primary motivations in life and it has a powerful impact on our emotions, finances, and relationships. For instance, becoming diabetic not only affects your body, it increases your medical expenses and can place limits on your social interactions.

Once you have finished looking at the benefits, the next question focuses your attention on the other side of the coin by considering the ramifications (the costs) of doing nothing. In many cases, doing nothing has negative consequences, but this is not always the case. Sometimes, doing nothing is not such a bad choice and may even have a greater appeal than trying to make changes. As with the previous question, you should consider the ramifications from the same four perspectives of; financial, emotional, relational, and physical consequences. You should also do your best to estimate a financial cost where possible. It can be difficult and sometimes impossible to place a financial estimate on some benefits. This is to be expected. But when possible, identifying a financial estimate, even a guess- timate, will help in determining whether the performance gap is worth doing anything about.

Once you have documented all the benefits, ramifications, and costs, you are in a better position to more objectively decide whether the performance gap is worth doing anything about. In the final question of this step, you will be asked to make that decision. Sometimes the decision to continue will be clear, and sometimes you may determine that it's just not worth doing anything about. In the latter case, STOP! There is no need to go any further in the process. Of course, just because it is not worth doing anything about right now does not mean it won't become more important later. We live in a busy world and we often need to prioritize our time and resources, so, occasionally, you may want to revisit the performance at a later date and can indicate this on the worksheet.

DEMONSTRATION

In the Customer Service Agents example below, you can see the benefits and costs that were identified in questions 9 and 10. Of these, the benefit of maintaining the accuracy of the customer data and cost of processing orders or paperwork with incorrect data are potential mirror opposites. However, the financial estimate for the benefit was left blank because the data was already supposed to be accurate. Making it accurate did not really bring any added benefit.

Is it Worth Doing Anything About?

9. What benefits (financial, emotional, relational, and/or physical) will be realized if the performance expectation is achieved? *Be Specific.*

BENEFITS	Manage existing customer calls
	Maintain accuracy of customer data
	Positive relationship between management and agents

10. If you do nothing to improve the performance, what will be the financial, emotional, relational, and/or physical ramifications or costs? *Be Specific.*

COSTS	Inaccurately processed orders due to incorrect customer data (About 2 million per year)
	Unhappy customers
	Poor relationship between management and agents
	Expectations for quotas may continue to increase unrealistically

11. Given the information above, is it worth doing anything about right now?

     ☒ **YES**: Continue to the question #12
     ❏ **NO**: **STOP** and/or set a date that you may want to revisit this gap

Turning our attention from the benefits to the costs, one of the four that was identified stood out and was easier to place a financial estimate on. Since the data had become increasingly inaccurate, the company had already started incurring some additional expense and stood to incur more if the problem continued. These added costs could be estimated for potential financial loss of $2 million in one year. Based on this information, the final question was determined to be a solid YES. We determined that the performance gap was worth doing something about right away and we continued to complete the rest of the worksheet.

Your Turn!

Stop and take a few minutes to document the benefits and costs of achieving the expected performance you identified in your practice

---

SECTION 2: CAUSES AND SOLUTIONS

Now that you have collected your foundational information and focused your thinking about the performance, the "Causes and Solutions" section of the worksheet is designed to help you identify the causes of the gap and to start developing potential solutions that target those causes. This section is broken into three steps that follow the understanding that all performance gaps are caused by Hills, Skills, and Wills.

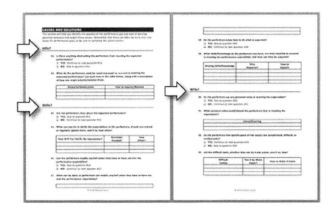

As you progress through the section, you will need to remember that many performance gaps can be caused by more than one of the three gaps, so even if you identify a cause in the first focus area, you should continue answering all the questions and steps to make sure you have considered all the possibilities.

STEP 5: HILLS?

The first step in this section addresses potential Hill gaps by asking if there is anything obstructing the performers from meeting the expected performance. If the answer is NO, you will have ruled out one of the three causes of gaps and can skip ahead to assessing the next one. However, if you or those you interview answered YES, you will be directed to the next question, which starts the process of targeted problem solving by seeking to identify those obstacles and how they might be removed or overcome.

DEMONSTRATION

In the Customer Service example, no additional resources were initially identified or reported as being an obstruction, but as more people were interviewed it became clear that this was not correct.

Hills

12. Is there anything obstructing the performers from meeting the expected performance?

    ☒ **YES**: Continue to next question #13
    ❑ **NO**: Skip to question #14

13. What do the performers need (or need removed) to succeed in meeting the expected performance? List each item in the table below, along with a description of how you might acquire/remove them.

Resource/Obstruction	How to Acquire/Remove
~~Operation metrics policy: unrealistic expectation for call quotas~~	~~Reduce call quotas~~
Time: increased call quotas have reduced time to complete other tasks	Work longer; remove or transfer tasks to other workers; reduce call quotas

As you can see above, there were two obstacles that became clear. The operational expectations for call quotas were said by most of the Agents to be an obstacle, and all indicated that more time was sorely needed. The other comments about the operations policy were struck out because the policy was only obstructive due to a lack of time. The policy could still be an issue but time was the root issue. Whether the policy obstruction was struck out or not, two Hills were identified that otherwise may have been overlooked. Having identified them allowed us to develop some potential solutions that were very targeted.

Your Turn!

Stop and take a few minutes to determine whether any Hills may be causing your performance gap. Complete this step on the worksheet you've already started.

STEP 6: Skills?

After determining whether the performance is affected by any Hill gaps, the next step turns your attention on whether or not the performers have all the knowledge and skills needed to meet the expected performance. The first question (#14) begins with asking whether or not they even know what is expected of them. As discussed in the previous chapter, understanding the expectation is the first piece that knowledge performers need in order to be successful. After all, how can someone meet an expectation if they don't know what it is or that one exists? If the performers do not know what the expectation is, the next question (#15) will lead you to identify ways to make it clear to them. It also encourages those involved to consider whether clarifying the expectation is something that should be done repeatedly, and if so, how often. If, however, the performers know what is expected, you will be directed to skip ahead (to question #16) and determine whether the performers know when they have met the expectation or how far they are from meeting it. As with the previous two questions, answering YES will direct you to the next question (#17), which asks you to list what might be done to correct this. On the other hand, if performers are aware of just how well or poor their progress toward meeting the expectation is, you will be directed to skip ahead (to question #18) and address the final set of question for this step.

After addressing the performer's awareness of the expectation and their ability to measure their progress toward it, the final questions address all the other pieces of knowledge or skill that might be missing. Frequently, skills center on technical knowledge or ability, such as a nurse knowing how to take someone's pulse or a mechanic knowing how to operate a certain piece of machinery. But, it can also relate to other types of knowledge and abilities, such as speaking a foreign language or knowing when it would be inappropriate to make a joke. Do the performers know how to do what is expected? If the answer to this question is YES, you're done and will be directed to the next step. If your answer is no however, you will need to proceed to the final question in this step. Here you will need to begin listing all the missing skills or knowledge that is required to meet the expectation and some potential solutions to target them each. This is one of the more critical places to make sure you involve others. Involving others will go a long way in making sure you don't overlook any required skills or knowledge performers need to be successful. If able, you may want to involve a skilled performance analyst or instructional designer in this step. The reason for this is that the people closest to a problem or most skilled in a particular task will miss things simply because it comes so naturally to them. A skilled performance analyst or instructional designer will know how to keep this from happening.

DEMONSTRATION

Let's review how this played out in the Customer Service example. In asking the first question, it was clear the Agents knew what was expected of them. This directed us to skip question #15.

Skills?

14. Are the performers clear about the expected performance?

    ☒ **YES**: Skip to question #16
    ❑ **NO**: Continue to next question #15

15. What can you do to clarify the expectations to the performers, should you remind or regularly update them, and if so, how often?

How Will You Clarify the Expectation?	Reminder Needed?	How Often?

16. Can the performers readily see/tell when they have or have not met the performance expectation?

    ☒ **YES**: Skip to question #18
    ❑ **NO**: Continue to next question #17

17. What can be done so performers can readily see/tell when they have or have not met the performance expectation?

_____
_____
_____

18. Do the performers know how to do what is expected?

    ☒ **YES**: Skip to question #20
    ❑ **NO**: Continue to next question #19

19. What skills/knowledge do the performers not have, are they required to succeed in meeting the performance expectation, and how can they be acquired?

Missing Skills/Knowledge	Why Required?	How to Acquire

Moving to the next question (#16), the Agents also received regular reports telling them how they were performing against the expectations and, according to the worksheet, this response directed us to skip question #17. In asking question #18, the Agents actually proved that they had all the knowledge and skills needed to complete the call logs correctly, and the training manager nearly admitted as much once she was pressed on the question. Based on this response there was no need to address the last question and the step was concluded.

HILLS, SKILLS, AND WILLS

Your Turn!
Stop and consider whether there may be any missing skills or knowledge required to achieve the expected performance in your practice worksheet.

STEP 7: WILLS?

If not A or B, then the answer must be C. If you have concluded that there are no Hill or Skill gaps causing the performers to fail in meeting the expected performance, the logical conclusion is that you have a Will gap. However, if you did identify a missing Hill or Skill, you may still have Will issues contributing to the gap in performance. You should not cut the process short here. Cutting the performance assessment process short could result in a partial increase in performance, but unresolved Will gaps tend to limit or wipe out any long term success. The final step in the "Causes and Solutions" section will guide you in identifying potential Will gaps and developing some targeted solutions to address them. It does this by determining whether the performers:

1. Find worth in meeting the expectation
2. Find any of the task required to meet the expectation too difficult
3. Are being punished when they do met the expectation
4. Are being rewarded when they do not meet the expectation.

As discussed in Chapter 5, humans need to be able to see some value or meaning behind their actions or their motivation and performance suffers. Since Will gaps are all about the performer's willingness to meet an expectation, based on the worth they see in it, the first question (#20) begins by determining whether the performers do or do not find any value or meaning in what they are expected to do. If the answer is YES, you will be directed to skip ahead (to question #22). But, if the answer is NO, you need to think through and document the value or meaning that could/would/should resonate with them and incorporate a way to communicate this in your overall performance improvement plan.

Once this has been done, the next two questions look at whether the expected performance is perceived as too difficult or cumbersome. Of course, difficulty does not mean that performers will not meet the expectations, but difficulty tends to decrease motivation while simplification tends to improve it. The first of these two questions (#22) asks if there are any tasks that are too difficult. Obviously, if the performers perceive the tasks as too difficult, you should seek to identify what those tasks are. You should

88

also consider whether they can be made easier and how that might be accomplished, this is the purpose of the next question (#23). Once these are completed, you can proceed to the final four questions in this step

The last four questions in this step address our final two Will killers. The first is whether the performers are, or believe they would be, negatively affected by doing what is expected. Punishing performers for doing the right thing is a rarely intended but not an uncommon situation, and one that will surely impact their Wills. A common example of this is when employees stop sharing or participating in team meetings because whenever they share an idea or solution, they are made responsible for carrying it out. If you answer YES to the question about punishing performance (#24) you will be directed to the next one (#25). Here you will seek to document all the negative effects, real or perceived, and identify ways to remove them. If however, the performers do not believe they are, or would be, negatively affected you can skip ahead to consider positive consequences for not doing what is expected (question #26). In this question you are primarily looking for things that reward behaviors you do not want. Consider the example we just discussed. If the expected performance is for people to share ideas in the meeting, handing out gift cards to everyone that comes rewards the wrong thing. People may come but they still won't share ideas. If you determine that the performers are not being rewarded when they don't meet the expectation, you are done with this step. However, a YES response to the question will prompt you to complete the last one in the step (#27). Here you are asked to document all the positive effects, real or perceived, and identify ways to remove them.

DEMONSTRATION

In the Customer Service example, the first question revealed that the Agents did not find any personal value or meaning in meeting the new expectation. A few of the performers were aware of the general importance in having updated data in the systems but they were much more interested in getting their work done on time, and most had not really thought about any meaningful reasons to meet the expectation. Based on the response to the first question, the worksheet directed us to question #21. Here, though it took some serious prompting to get most to find any, we were able to identify a few items of personal value or meaning to the Agents. The meaningfulness of helping others was one such idea that many found to be highly valuable but did not often think about. In addition, the potential loss of their jobs was something that only some managers thought might motivate the Agent to be more diligent in their documentation.

Wills?

20. Do the performers see any personal value in meeting the expectation?

    ❑ **YES**: Skip to question #22
    ☒ **NO**: Continue to next question #21

21. What personal value could/should the performers find in meeting the expectation?

Value/Meaning
May lead to job loss
To be someone that provides help and comfort to others who are already struggling with medical situations
Be seen and rewarded as a high performing employee

22. Do the performers find specific parts of the task(s) too complicated, difficult, or cumbersome?

    ☒ **YES**: Continue to next question #23
    ❑ **NO**: Skip to question #24

23. List the difficult tasks, whether they can be made easier, and if so, how?

Difficult Task(s)	Can it be Made Easier?	How to Make it Easier
Completing all fields and continuing to meet new call quotas	Yes	Need more time; Decrease call quota

24. Do the performers experience, or anticipate, any negative consequences (physical, emotional, financial, etc.) if they do what is expected?

    ☒ **YES**: Continue to next question #25
    ❑ **NO**: Skip to question #26

25. List any negative consequences experienced or anticipated by the performers when they do what is expected, identify if they can be removed, and how you might remove them

Negative Consequences	How to Remove it
Not able to answer/handle as many calls each day which leads to job loss	Pay for extra work hours; Reassess and adjust call quotas; Don't fire for missing quotas

26. Do the performers experience, or anticipate, any positive consequences (physical, emotional, financial, etc.) when they do not do what is expected?

    ☒ **YES**: Continue to next question #27
    ❏ **NO**: Skip to question #28 (Next Section)

27. List any positive consequences experienced or anticipated by the performers when they do less than what is expected and how you might remove them.

Positive Consequences	How to Remove it
Their manager is happy with them	Manager share concern/disappointment with them when missing quotas
Able to meet quotas/metrics that received the most attention	Place equal importance on quality of data as # of call handled
Keep jobs	Fire for missing quotas

Looking at the difficulty of the tasks (in question #22) many of the Agents mentioned that the expectation itself was too difficult (not the specific tasks within the expectation). It is easy for people to speak in generalities, so you will need to encourage the performer you are interviewing to be specific about the tasks that are actually required to meet the expectation. In this case, the individual tasks required to meet the log and quota expectations were not thought to be too difficult. The difficulty was the overall expectation and how long it took to achieve it.

Moving on to the next question (#24), whether the Agent's experienced, or thought they would experience, any negative consequences when they did meet the expectation. All the Agents were unanimous in responding YES. Taking the time to complete the required call log fields correctly would take more time and would end up decreasing the number of calls they were able to handle. Since missing the call quota was perceived to be a sure way to get fired, they were not willing to or interested in taking this risk. To correct this consequence three potential solutions were proposed:

1. Pay for extra work hours
2. Reassess and adjust call quotas
3. Stop firing employees for missing quotas.

In moving to the last two questions in this step, the Agents were asked whether they experienced any positive consequences for not meeting the expectation. Interestingly, their answers clearly revealed that they did. A few Agents mentioned that how focusing on meeting the quotas kept their manager happy with them, but nearly all mentioned that their inattention to completing all the log fields allowed them to continue meeting the quotas and thereby avoid losing their jobs. As directed by the worksheet, each of these responses was documented in question #27, as were their potential solutions.

SECTION 3: DEFINING YOUR PLAN

"Defining your Plan" is the final section of the worksheet. It is designed to take the information you have captured, regarding the performance gap, and to finalize it into a workable plan. While there is some additional work to do, the main focus in this section is made up of three steps:
1. Review the information you have already gathered
2. Select the solutions that would best fit the context
3. Give consideration to various needs associated with implementation of the plan itself.

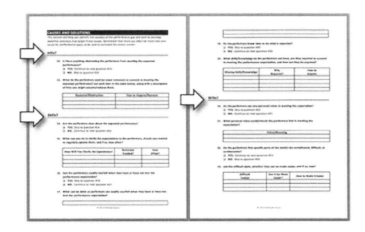

STEP 8: Assess Your Solutions

This step in the worksheet (#28) begins by reviewing all the solutions you have identified for each performance gap. To do this, you are directed to transfer the gap solutions you identified in Section 2 into one table and try to estimate a financial cost associated with each solution. The table points you to the appropriate questions for each gap and solution. If you were directed to skip questions earlier and did not need to develop any solutions, or if the potential solutions do not have any financial cost, it is perfectly acceptable to leave those areas blank. But, identifying the cost of your solutions will have an important impact on your selection process, so don't treat this step lightly. Once the solutions have been reviewed and you have done your best to estimate costs, the next question (#29) will ask you to refer back to the Benefits/Costs answers you gave in the initial section of your analysis (questions #9 and #10). You will need to review these, and estimate financial costs associated for them if you have not already done so.

Again, the importance in this is to help you assess which solutions will best achieve your expectations and avoid unnecessary costs.

From here, the next step (#30) will direct you to identify which solutions you believe should be applied and/or which should be ignored based on the information you have gathered and reviewed. You can do this by simply striking out certain solutions and highlighting others. If you don't like this approach, find another that works well for you. The key point to remember in this step is that the "best" outcome should always be more worthwhile than doing nothing, and that does not mean it will always cost less. This step will also direct you to document any additional solutions that you believe would be beneficial but were not specifically already identified in the assessment.

The final step in this section and in the entire worksheet (#31) is simply a prompt to get you thinking about some important aspects related to implementing all the hard work you have just completed. It prompts you to consider the people, timing, sequence, and measures of success for your plan. This may actually be something that others will manage now that you have finished your analysis, however, there are often insights you can provide that will help with these decisions, such as the order in which the solutions should be implemented or how best to measure progress in achieving each solution. If you are responsible for implementing the performance improvement you will need to consider each of the items in this list. If you are not responsible, don't check out until you have provided some thought to those who are.

DEMONSTRATION

In the Customer Service example, the first step (#28) shows how the solutions were carried over from the previous sections and in some cases reworded to read more clearly. The Benefits and Ramifications were also transferred over (#29) and cost estimates were determined for each solution, as much as possible. Since the table only shows the estimated cost, it is particularly important when handling business performance to have backup documentation regarding how these estimates were determined.

Assess Your Solutions

28. Review the information you collected in the previous section (questions 12 – 27), add them in the table below, and estimate the cost of implementing each solution.

Issue and Type?	Solutions	Cost Estimate
Hills: Resources to Acquire (Q13)	Need more time: Work longer;	$500K p/yr
	Need more time: remove or transfer tasks to other workers	$250K p/yr
	Need more time: reduce call quotas	$0 p/yr
Skills: Clarify Expectations (Q15)		
Skills: Provide Performance Feedback (Q17)		
Skills: Knowledge/ Skills to Acquire (Q19)		
Wills: Meaning (Q21)	Communicating that continuing to ignore may lead to job loss	$0 p/yr
	Communicating the value of being someone that provides help and comfort to others who are already struggling with medical situations	$0 p/yr
	Communicating and/or rewarding people as a high performing employees when meeting expectation	$0 - 100K p/yr
Wills: Tasks to Simplify (Q23)	Need more time	See Neg Consequences
	Decrease call quota	See Neg Consequences
Wills: Negative Consequences to Remove (Q25)	Pay for extra work hours	500K p/yr
	Reassess and adjust call quotas	$5K p/yr
	Don't fire for missing quotas	$0 p/yr

Issue and Type?	Solutions	Cost Estimate
Wills: Positive Consequences to Remove (Q27)	Manager share concern/disappointment with them when missing quotas	$0 p/yr
	Place equal importance on quality of data as # of call handled	$0 p/yr
	Fire for missing quotas	$12K p/yr (new hires)
Other Solutions (Q30)	Ensure Agents are aware of the potential cost to the company for having inaccurate data (~$2M)	$0 p/yr
	Provide feedback mechanism between management and agents to better assess quotas expectations	$5K p/yr

29. Consider the benefits/ramifications identified in Section 1 (questions 9-10) and list them in the tables below with a $$ estimate for each (as appropriate). Also add any new benefits/ramifications now that your analysis is nearly completed.

Benefits of Improved Performance	$$ Estimate
Manage existing customer calls	NA
Maintain accuracy of customer data	See costs below
Positive relationship between management and agents	NA

Ramifications for Doing Nothing	$$ Estimate
Inaccurately processed orders due to incorrect customer data)	~2M p/yr
Unhappy customers	?
Poor relationship between management and agents	NA
Expectations for quotas may continue to increase unrealistically	?

Select Your Solution(s)

30. Which solutions will best target the performance gaps and improve performance? Highlight or mark the solutions in the table above (question 28) and include any additional solutions that may not have been accounted for.

   NOTE: The "best" outcome should always be more worthwhile than doing nothing, but that does not mean it will always cost less.

Planning to Implement

31. Now that you know the cause(s) of your performance gap and what to do about them, consider the following items as you finalize your performance improvement plan. Then begin implementing and monitoring your progress.

   - ❏ Who will be responsible for making sure each solution is implemented?
   - ❏ In what order will the solution(s) be implemented?
   - ❏ When will each solution begin implementation?
   - ❏ When will each solution be fully implemented?
   - ❏ How will progress for each solution be measured?
   - ❏ How will each solution be maintained?

As all the solutions, benefits, and costs were captured in the table, the next step (#30) was simply to decide which would best fit and be recommended for implementation. As instructed by the worksheet, we highlighted the solutions in the table (#28) and included a few others that aligned with the analysis results. In particular, ensuring that Agents were keenly aware that the cost to the company for having inaccurate data was estimated at $2 million per year, and providing a feedback mechanism between management and agents to ensure future quota expectations were given a reality check. With all this completed, the last step of planning the implementation (#31) was carried out by a team of other individuals in the department and the performance analyst was consulted for their opinions.

Your Turn!
Assess the solutions you identified and complete your practice worksheet.

Having walked through the entire HSW Performance Analysis Worksheet, I hope you could see how it incorporates all the aspects of the Hill, Skill, Will methodology addressed in this book. More importantly, I hope you found it relatively easy to follow and now feel more prepared to improve your performance or the performance of others. Like anything worthwhile, it takes time and practice. But, even if you only uncover one gap that you would have overlooked, or avoid investing in one solution that didn't target the real cause of the gap follows method, the savings in money, time, and headaches will have been well worth it.

CONCLUSION AND NEXT STEPS

Hills, Skills, and Wills is a powerful performance improvement guide because it frames your focus on all the potential causes of performance gaps in a simple and memorable way.

> # THINK YOU
> # YOU CAN'T
> # BE FOOLED?
> **You probably just were. Read it again!**

Were you fooled by the above statement? Did you read or skip the extra "you?" I took this example from a recent National Geographic television show called Brain Games. The program explores the different ways in which the human brain processes information and how it can affect our behavior. I included it here to illustrate two final points before we wrap things up. The first is how easy it can be for us to take shortcuts.

Every day we are bombarded with thousands of pieces of information that we use to make choices and decisions but, while the human brain is capable of storing enormous amounts, it does not always process that information as we might expect or want. Our brain takes shortcuts, and so do we. When faced with performance problems, many people often just go with the first (or any) solution that seems to make some logical sense. The time pressure to produce results more quickly (a Hill), being unfamiliar about a particular subject (a Skill), or having an ego the size of Texas (a Will) will often cause people to go with the first logical solution, or a solution that they like, instead of examining the situation more closely to ensure they haven't missed anything. If you doubt this, just do some research on the response rate of people that purchase infomercial products.

The "Can you be fooled?" test also illustrates a second point, that these shortcuts can be both useful and detrimental. Skipping the extra "you" was very efficient of your brain, as it saved you from wasting a millisecond of your time. On the other hand, if you were an editor, missing the duplicate word could be a serious problem. Likewise, taking shortcuts when analyzing performance gaps can be both useful and a detriment. Throughout the book I have discussed how detrimental a superficial response to performance problems can be but, to be honest, there is a flip side. Responding quickly with a solution can be what gives you a competitive advantage in a situation.

The more I have worked with businesses, the more I have heard this need for "fast action" used as a reason to shortcut the analysis process. "We can't afford to get stuck in Analysis Paralysis," is the phrase commonly used, and they are partly right. Time is a commodity and an effective performance analyst, or process, cannot afford to ignore that. In conducting your performance analysis, you need to be sound in your approach and sensitive to the importance of time.

Typically, people get stuck in Analysis Paralysis because they are fearful of making a poor decision and want to do all they can to decrease that potential. But, there are other reasons. Sometimes people already have a solution in mind and get stuck because they keep trying to prove that it is the right one (even if it is isn't). As you examine the areas you want to improve performance you should be aware of these traps. You should also be aware that not all claims of Analysis Paralysis are accurate. Sometimes people will be directed to keep doing more analysis and then be blamed for it taking so long. This frequently happens when others want to look like they are trying to move forward but, in reality, they actually want to delay or avoid making any decisions as long as possible. One of the more obvious examples of this is in the words and inaction of politicians running for public office. Another false claim of Analysis Paralysis occurs when people shortcut the performance analysis because the results are starting to contradict the outcomes they are looking for. On one occasion I even heard a business leader say that further analysis was not needed because "people can always find different opinions or results" so there is really no reason to look at it further.

The fact is, there needs to be a balance. A balance between "Analysis Paralysis" and what I call "The Reaction Faction," those who react without really knowing or caring much about the situation and expected results. Where is that balance? The best answer I can give would probably be to say the time spent analyzing the performance should be proportional to the impact of any decisions. The Hills, Skills, and Wills framework and worksheet are simple and allow you to avoid Analysis Paralysis while still making sure you don't overlook critical aspects of the performance.

NEXT STEPS

While I hope you found the insights, stories, and tools provided in the book to be thought provoking and helpful in your performance improvement endeavors, they are in no way an exhaustive accounting of what is available on the topic. At the start of the book I made a pledge that, by the end, you would not only be able to look at any performance gap and quickly identify what has been keeping you from being able to change it, but you would be able to create a plan that specifically targeted those causes and help you, or your organization, succeed in achieving the performance you so desired or needed. With this pledge (expectation) in mind, we covered the following list of the subjects. Review the list and check off those that you feel you have good handle on.

- ◻ Provided an overview of the book (Ch. 1)
- ◻ Explored whether this book was right for you (Ch.1)
- ◻ Explained who I am and my interest in the subject (Ch. 1)
- ◻ Defined and discussed performance, performance improvement, and the connection between it and behavioral expectations. (Ch. 2)
- ◻ Explained how performance improvement requires behavioral change (Ch. 2)
- ◻ Demonstrated what can happen when people do not properly assess performance gaps (Ch. 2)
- ◻ Showed how humans are uniquely suited to change (Ch. 3)
- ◻ Challenged you to decide whether you believe people can and do change (Ch. 3)
- ◻ Explored common areas that people say can't be

changed (Ch. 3)

- Demonstrated how few things there are that cannot be changed (Ch. 3)
- Provided real life examples of change (Ch. 3)
- Defined and explained Hills, Skills, and Wills. (Ch.4)
- Showed how correctly identifying these is the key to performance improvement (Ch. 4)
- Provided you an opportunity to practice identifying
- Hill, Skill, and Will gaps (Ch. 4)
- Shared two true stories that demonstrated how Hill, Skill, and Will gaps play out in real life. (Ch. 5)
- Identified and explored several approaches to resolving Hill, Skill, and Will gaps (Ch. 6)
- Explained that performance gap analysis is a process (Ch. 7)
- Provided three pointers when following any performance analysis process (Ch. 7)
- Explained how to use the HSW worksheet (Ch. 7)
- Walked through an example of using the HSW worksheet (Ch. 7)
- Provided you the opportunity to practice using the HSW worksheet on your own performance improvement needs (Ch. 7)

For those where you don't feel as confident, go back and review them again. Most importantly, practice using the methodology and the HSW Performance Analysis Worksheet. The more you use it, the more you proficient you will become in spotting situations where critical root causes are being overlooked or ignored. By identifying and addressing these, you can improve your own performance and the performance of others.

Now, I could simply assume I have achieved my expectation (pledge) and end the book here but as I have said before, I am a "Show Me" kind of guy and what I say doesn't really matter. They're just words on paper until you see and experience it for yourself. Even though I gave you opportunities to practice, some of you will need more time to think on and experiment with it. As such, I cannot really conclude the book. Rather, I have to treat this more as a checkpoint, a place where I can figuratively pass on the baton and have each of you run with it for a while.

To facilitate this, I have decided to leverage the power of social media technologies. This idea is to use it as a living laboratory. A place where we all get to play the role of a performance scientist, conducting our own experiments and sharing our results with others. Here we can work together to reinforce, disprove, refine, and/or revise what has been learned and how to apply it in the real world. This site will also provide access to blank copies of the HSW Performance Analysis Worksheet and other useful documents as they are shared.

What will my role be? The same as yours! While I will participate and update some information at the site, I do not intend to overly manage the posts, comments, and suggestions provided by others. The site is intended to be a place of pure uncensored ideas, experiences, and suggestions. This is the environment I believe will provide the most honest and most robust stage for testing and improving upon what I have shared in the book.

As we all grow in our understanding and ability to improve performance, I expect that the site too will evolve and grow as well. Your input will play a major role in this. You can access and join the online community at:

https://www.facebook.com/HillsSkillsWills

If you have gone through the trouble of reading the entire book, I truly hope you will experiment with it and share your results online. I wish you all the best in your performance improvement efforts and look forward to hearing what you discover for yourself.

APPENDIX A

HSW Performance Analysis Worksheet

GETTING STARTED

This section will help you collect some foundational information that is essential before trying to determine the cause or solutions of the performance gap. It will focus your thinking and actions throughout the rest of the worksheet and performance analysis process.

What's the Gap?

1. Describe the performance you are expecting? Be specific.

2. Describe the performance that is actually taking place? Be specific.

3. Describe the performance gap (the difference between the expected and actual performance).

Who Does it Affect?

4. List the names, titles, or types of people that are affected by the performance, which have been involved in the analysis, and in what capacity?

	Names, Titles, or Typs of People	Interviewed?
Performers		
Decision Makers		
Recipients of Performance		

Is it Possible?

5. Have the performers ever met the performance expectation?

❑ **YES**: Skip ahead and answer question #8A
❑ **NO**: Continue to next question #6

6. Has anyone, anywhere or anytime, ever been successful in meeting the performance expectation?

❑ **YES**: Skip ahead and answer question #8A
❑ **NO**: Continue to next question #7

7. Do you believe the performance expectation can be met?

❑ **YES**: Answer question #8B
❑ **NO** or **NOT SURE**: Answer question #8B

8. A) What has changed since the performance was last achieved? B) Why do/don't you believe the performance expectation can be met?

Is it Worth Doing Anything About?

9. What benefits (financial, emotional, relational, and/or physical) will be realized if the performance expectation is achieved? *Be Specific.*

BENEFITS	

10. If you do nothing to improve the performance, what will be the financial, emotional, relational, and/or physical ramifications or costs? *Be Specific.*

COSTS	

11. Given the information above, is it worth doing anything about right now?

- ❑ **YES**: Continue to the question #12
- ❑ **NO**: **STOP** and/or set a date that you may want to revisit this gap

CAUSES AND SOLUTIONS

This section will help you identify the cause(s) of the performance gap and start to develop potential solutions that target those causes. Remember that there can often be more than one cause for performance gaps, so be sure to complete the entire section.

Hills

12. Is there anything obstructing the performers from meeting the expected performance?

- ❑ **YES**: Continue to next question #13
- ❑ **NO**: Skip to question #14

13. What do the performers need (or need removed) to succeed in meeting the expected performance? List each item in the table below, along with a description of how you might acquire/remove them.

Resource/Obstruction	How to Acquire/Remove

Skills?

14. Are the performers clear about the expected performance?

   ❑ **YES**: Skip to question #16
   ❑ **NO**: Continue to next question #15

15. What can you do to clarify the expectations to the performers, should you remind or regularly update them, and if so, how often?

How Will You Clarify the Expectation?	Reminder Needed?	How Often?

16. Can the performers readily see/tell when they have or have not met the performance expectation?

   ❑ **YES**: Skip to question #18
   ❑ **NO**: Continue to next question #17

17. What can be done so performers can readily see/tell when they have or have not met the performance expectation?

18. Do the performers know how to do what is expected?

   ❑ **YES**: Skip to question #20
   ❑ **NO**: Continue to next question #19

19. What skills/knowledge do the performers not have, are they required to succeed in meeting the performance expectation, and how can they be acquired?

Missing Skills/Knowledge	Why Required?	How to Acquire

Wills?

20. Do the performers see any personal value in meeting the expectation?

    - ❑ **YES**: Skip to question #22
    - ❑ **NO**: Continue to next question #21

21. What personal value could/should the performers find in meeting the expectation?

Value/Meaning

22. Do the performers find specific parts of the task(s) too complicated, difficult, or cumbersome?

    - ❑ **YES**: Continue to next question #23
    - ❑ **NO**: Skip to question #24

23. List the difficult tasks, whether they can be made easier, and if so, how?

Difficult Task(s)	Can it be Made Easier?	How to Make it Easier

24. Do the performers experience, or anticipate, any negative consequences (physical, emotional, financial, etc.) if they do what is expected?

    - ❑ **YES**: Continue to next question #25
    - ❑ **NO**: Skip to question #26

25. List any negative consequences experienced or anticipated by the performers when they do what is expected, identify if they can be removed, and how you might remove them

Negative Consequences	How to Remove it

26. Do the performers experience, or anticipate, any positive consequences (physical, emotional, financial, etc.) when they do not do what is expected?

    - ❑ **YES**: Continue to next question #27
    - ❑ **NO**: Skip to question #28 (Next Section)

27. List any positive consequences experienced or anticipated by the performers when they do less than what is expected and how you might remove them.

Positive Consequences	How to Remove it

DEFINE YOUR PLAN

This section will help you in selecting the most appropriate solutions and how to get started implementing them.

Assess Your Solutions

28. Review the information you collected in the previous section (questions 12 – 27), add them in the table below, and estimate the cost of implementing each solution.

Issue and Type?	Solutions	Cost Estimate

29. Consider the benefits/ramifications identified in Section 1 (questions 9-10) and list them in the tables below with a $$ estimate for each (as appropriate). Also add any new benefits/ramifications now that your analysis is nearly completed.

Benefits of Improved Performance	$$ Estimate

Ramifications for Doing Nothing	$$ Estimate

Select Your Solution(s)

30. Which solutions will best target the performance gaps and improve performance? Highlight or mark the solutions in the table above (question 28) and include any additional solutions that may not have been accounted for.

   NOTE: The "best" outcome should always be more worthwhile than doing nothing, but that does not mean it will always cost less.

Planning to Implement

31. Now that you know the cause(s) of your performance gap and what to do about them, consider the following items as you finalize your performance improvement plan. Then begin implementing and monitoring your progress.

   ❑ Who will be responsible for making sure each solution is implemented?
   ❑ In what order will the solution(s) be implemented?
   ❑ When will each solution begin implementation?
   ❑ When will each solution be fully implemented?
   ❑ How will progress for each solution be measured?
   ❑ How will each solution be maintained?

APPENDIX B

HSW Performance Analysis Worksheet

GETTING STARTED

This section will help you collect some foundational information that is essential before trying to determine the cause or solutions of the performance gap. It will focus your thinking and actions throughout the rest of the worksheet and performance analysis process.

What's the Gap?

1. Describe the performance you are expecting? Be specific.

   > ~~Customer Services Agents need to complete their call logs.~~
   > Customer Services Agents need to handle 40 calls each day AND ensure all the required fields are completed in each call log.

2. Describe the performance that is actually taking place? Be specific.

   > ~~Customer Services Agents are not completing their call logs.~~ Customer Services Agents are handling 40 calls each day but several required fields in the call logs are being left incomplete or blank.

3. Describe the performance gap (the difference between the expected and actual performance).

   > ~~Customer Services Agents need to complete their call logs.~~ Customer Services Agents need to complete all required fields in their call logs.

Who Does it Affect?

4. List the names, titles, or types of people that are affected by the performance, which have been involved in the analysis, and in what capacity?

	Names, Titles, or Typs of People	Interviewed?
Performers	100 Customer Service Agents	Interviewed (10)
Decision Makers	Training Manager	Interviewed and Re-viewed Analysis
	Agent Manager	Interviewed and Re-viewed Analysis
	Audit Manager	Interviewed and Re-viewed Analysis
	Call Center Manager	Interviewed and Re-viewed Analysis
	VP Operations	Reviewed Analysis
Recipients of Performance	Customers	

Is it Possible?

5. Have the performers ever met the performance expectation?

   - ☐ **YES**: Skip ahead and answer question #8A
   - ☒ **NO**: Continue to next question #6

6. Has anyone, anywhere or anytime, ever been successful in meeting the performance expectation?

   - ☐ **YES**: Skip ahead and answer question #8A
   - ☒ **NO**: Continue to next question #7

7. Do you believe the performance expectation can be met?

   - ☐ **YES**: Answer question #8B
   - ☒ **NO** or **NOT SURE**: Answer question #8B

8. A) What has changed since the performance was last achieved? B) Why do/don't you believe the performance expectation can be met?

   > Not sure it can be met. Never met before. Most Agents do not believe the expectation is realistic. Agents have met all previous expectations but have repeatedly complained about **increasing call quotas. Not enough time** for calls and all other tasks.

Is it Worth Doing Anything About?

9. What benefits (financial, emotional, relational, and/or physical) will be realized if the performance expectation is achieved? *Be Specific.*

BENEFITS	Manage existing customer calls
	Maintain accuracy of customer data
	Positive relationship between management and agents

10. If you do nothing to improve the performance, what will be the financial, emotional, relational, and/or physical ramifications or costs? *Be Specific.*

COSTS	Inaccurately processed orders due to incorrect customer data (About 2 million per year)
	Unhappy customers
	Poor relationship between management and agents
	Expectations for quotas may continue to increase unrealistically

11. Given the information above, is it worth doing anything about right now?

    ☒ **YES**: Continue to the question #12
    ❑ **NO**: **STOP** and/or set a date that you may want to revisit this gap

CAUSES AND SOLUTIONS

This section will help you identify the cause(s) of the performance gap and start to develop potential solutions that target those causes. Remember that there can often be more than one cause for performance gaps, so be sure to complete the entire section.

Hills

12. Is there anything obstructing the performers from meeting the expected performance?

    ❑ **YES**: Continue to next question #13
    ☒ **NO**: Skip to question #14

13. What do the performers need (or need removed) to succeed in meeting the expected performance? List each item in the table below, along with a description of how you might acquire/remove them.

Resource/Obstruction	How to Acquire/Remove
~~Operation metrics policy: unrealistic expectation for call quotas~~	~~Reduce call quotas~~
Time: increased call quotas have reduced time to complete other tasks	Work longer; remove or transfer tasks to other workers; reduce call quotas

Skills?

14. Are the performers clear about the expected performance?

☒ **YES**: Skip to question #16
❑ **NO**: Continue to next question #15

15. What can you do to clarify the expectations to the performers, should you remind or regularly update them, and if so, how often?

How Will You Clarify the Expectation?	Reminder Needed?	How Often?

16. Can the performers readily see/tell when they have or have not met the performance expectation?

☒ **YES**: Skip to question #18
❑ **NO**: Continue to next question #17

17. What can be done so performers can readily see/tell when they have or have not met the performance expectation?

_____
_____
_____

18. Do the performers know how to do what is expected?

☒ **YES**: Skip to question #20
❑ **NO**: Continue to next question #19

19. What skills/knowledge do the performers not have, are they required to succeed in meeting the performance expectation, and how can they be acquired?

Missing Skills/Knowledge	Why Required?	How to Acquire

Wills?

20. Do the performers see any personal value in meeting the expectation?

    ❏ **YES**: Skip to question #22
    ☒ **NO**: Continue to next question #21

21. What personal value could/should the performers find in meeting the expectation?

Value/Meaning
May lead to job loss
To be someone that provides help and comfort to others who are already struggling with medical situations
Be seen and rewarded as a high performing employee

22. Do the performers find specific parts of the task(s) too complicated, difficult, or cumbersome?

    ❏ **YES**: Continue to next question #23
    ☒ **NO**: Skip to question #24

23. List the difficult tasks, whether they can be made easier, and if so, how?

Difficult Task(s)	Can it be Made Easier?	How to Make it Easier
Completing all fields and continuing to meet new call quotas	Yes	Need more time; Decrease call quota

24. Do the performers experience, or anticipate, any negative consequences (physical, emotional, financial, etc.) if they do what is expected?

    ☒ **YES**: Continue to next question #25
    ❏ **NO**: Skip to question #26

25. List any negative consequences experienced or anticipated by the performers when they do what is expected, identify if they can be removed, and how you might remove them

Negative Consequences	How to Remove it
Not able to answer/handle as many calls each day which leads to job loss	Pay for extra work hours; Reassess and adjust call quotas; Don't fire for missing quotas

26. Do the performers experience, or anticipate, any positive consequences (physical, emotional, financial, etc.) when they do not do what is expected?

☐ **YES**: Continue to next question #27
☒ **NO**: Skip to question #28 (Next Section)

27. List any positive consequences experienced or anticipated by the performers when they do less than what is expected and how you might remove them.

Positive Consequences	How to Remove it
Their manager is happy with them	Manager share concern/disappointment with them when missing quotas
Able to meet quotas/metrics that received the most attention	Place equal importance on quality of data as # of call handled
Keep jobs	Fire for missing quotas

DEFINE YOUR PLAN

This section will help you in selecting the most appropriate solutions and how to get started implementing them.

Assess Your Solutions

28. Review the information you collected in the previous section (questions 12 – 27), add them in the table below, and estimate the cost of implementing each solution.

Issue and Type?	Issue and Type?	Cost Estimate
Hills: Resources to Acquire (Q13)	Need more time: Work longer;	$500K p/yr
	Need more time: remove or transfer tasks to other workers	$250K p/yr
	Need more time: reduce call quotas	$0 p/yr
Skills: Clarify Expectations (Q15)		
Skills: Provide Performance Feedback (Q17)		
Skills: Knowledge/ Skills to Acquire (Q19)		

Issue and Type?	Issue and Type?	Cost Estimate
Wills: Meaning (Q21)	Communicating that continuing to ignore may lead to job loss	$0 p/yr
	Communicating the value of being someone that provides help and comfort to others who are already struggling with medical situations	$0 p/yr
	Communicating and/or rewarding people as a high performing employees when meeting expectation	$0 - 100K p/yr
Wills: Tasks to Simplify (Q23)	Need more time	See Neg Consequences
	Decrease call quota	See Neg Consequences
Wills: Negative Consequences to Remove (Q25)	Pay for extra work hours	500K p/yr
	Reassess and adjust call quotas	$5K p/yr
	Don't fire for missing quotas	$0 p/yr
Wills: Positive Consequences to Remove (Q27)	Manager share concern/disappointment with them when missing quotas	$0 p/yr
	Place equal importance on quality of data as # of call handled	$0 p/yr
	Fire for missing quotas	$12K p/yr (new hires)
Other Solutions (Q30)	Ensure Agents are aware of the potential cost to the company for having inaccurate data (~$2M)	$0 p/yr
	Provide feedback mechanism between management and agents to better assess quotas expectations	$5K p/yr

29. Consider the benefits/ramifications identified in Section 1 (questions 9-10) and list them in the tables below with a $$ estimate for each (as appropriate). Also add any new benefits/ramifications now that your analysis is nearly completed.

Benefits of Improved Performance	$$ Estimate
Manage existing customer calls	NA
Maintain accuracy of customer data	See costs below
Positive relationship between management and agents	NA

Ramifications for Doing Nothing	$$ Estimate
Inaccurately processed orders due to incorrect customer data)	~2M p/yr
Unhappy customers	?
Poor relationship between management and agents	NA
Expectations for quotas may continue to increase unrealistically	?

Select Your Solution(s)

30. Which solutions will best target the performance gaps and improve performance? Highlight or mark the solutions in the table above (question 28) and include any additional solutions that may not have been accounted for.

NOTE: The "best" outcome should always be more worthwhile than doing nothing, but that does not mean it will always cost less.

Planning to Implement

31. Now that you know the cause(s) of your performance gap and what to do about them, consider the following items as you finalize your performance improvement plan. Then begin implementing and monitoring your progress.

- ❏ Who will be responsible for making sure each solution is implemented?
- ❏ In what order will the solution(s) be implemented?
- ❏ When will each solution begin implementation?
- ❏ When will each solution be fully implemented?
- ❏ How will progress for each solution be measured?
- ❏ How will each solution be maintained?

Made in the USA
San Bernardino, CA
20 October 2013